SOCIAL REFORM MOVEMENTS

The
CIVIL RIGHTS MOVEMENT

CHARLES PATTERSON

Facts On File®

AN INFOBASE HOLDINGS COMPANY

The Civil Rights Movement

Copyright © 1995 by Charles Patterson

Facts On File, Inc.
460 Park Avenue South
New York, NY 10016

Library of Congress Cataloging-in-Publication Data

Patterson, Charles.
  The civil rights movement / Charles Patterson.
    p. cm. — (Social reform movements)
  Includes bibliographical references and index.
  ISBN 0-8160-2968-7
  1. Afro-Americans—Civil rights. 2. Civil rights movements—
United States—History—20th century. I. Title. II. Series.
E185.61P32 1995
323.1196′196073—dc20   95-3027

Facts On File books are available at special discounts when purchased
in bulk quantities for businesses, associations, institutions, or sales
promotions. Please contact our Special Sales Department in New York
at 212/683-2244 or 800/322-8755.

Text design by Fred Pusterla
Cover design by Nora Wertz
Printed in the United States of America

MP FOF 10 9 8 7 6 5 4 3 2 1

This book is printed on acid-free paper.

C O N T E N T S

P R E F A C E

The black struggle for freedom that erupted in the 1950s and 1960s—called the civil rights movement—was one of the most dramatic and inspiring periods in American history. Before the movement's victories in mid-twentieth century, American blacks had been denied their basic rights of citizenship, especially in the South where segregation was maintained by law and custom.

While the struggle of African Americans to win their freedom had been under way long before the mid-1950s, the civil rights movement as we now know it began with two important developments—the landmark 1954 Supreme Court decision in the *Brown v. Board of Education of Topeka* case that declared school segregation unconstitutional, and the successful 1955–56 bus boycott by the black community of Montgomery, Alabama.

The *Brown* decision, which invalidated the separate-but-equal doctrine handed down in the 1896 *Plessy v. Ferguson* Supreme Court case, paved the way for the integration of school systems in the South. The Supreme Court ruling gave hope to civil rights advocates determined to challenge segregation in the courts under the banner of the National Association for the Advancement of Colored People (NAACP). It also inspired blacks to believe that the nation could live up to its ideals of justice and fair treatment under the law.

The success of the Montgomery bus boycott created the momentum and set the tone for a decade of southern-based civil rights campaigns that changed the South and the nation forever. The boycott mobilized and organized the entire black population of Montgomery with great effectiveness and introduced nonviolent protest on a mass scale. It also brought to the fore a young Baptist minister, the Reverend Martin Luther King, Jr.

Inspired by the Montgomery bus boycott, other forms of resistance to the indignity and repression of segregation sprang up throughout the South—student sit-ins, freedom rides, civil rights campaigns in Albany and Birmingham, the march on Washington, voter registration drives and the march from Selma to

Montgomery that culminated in the historic Voting Rights Act of 1965. The act secured black voting rights by sending federal officials into the South to oversee voter registration.

As the 1960s progressed, the focus of the civil rights movement shifted away from the South to more national issues. Broader economic and political goals having to do with jobs, housing and poverty replaced the earlier objectives of desegregation and voting rights. Young urban blacks and civil rights groups like the Student Nonviolent Coordinating Committee (SNCC) shifted their platforms from nonviolent integration to black power and self-defense. Discontent with the powerlessness and poverty of ghetto life exploded in a series of violent urban eruptions that shocked the nation.

Civil rights remained the nation's major political issue during the presidencies of John F. Kennedy and Lyndon Johnson until the nation and the civil rights movement itself got caught up in, and became divided by, the controversy over the undeclared war in Vietnam. The civil rights movement inspired and served as a model for social protest movements that followed, such as the anti-war and women's movements.

In this survey of the civil rights movement, I follow its course into the early 1970s, knowing full well that any decision about where to end an account of the civil rights era must be arbitrary, since the struggle to overcome the country's legacy of racism is ongoing. Even when the political climate was not favorable to progress on the civil rights front during the Reagan and Bush administrations, for example, Congress passed the Voting Rights Act extension of 1982, the Fair Housing Amendments of 1988, and the Civil Rights Act of 1991. In that sense, the civil rights movement is never over.

CHAPTER **One**

BACKGROUND
The Legacy of Slavery

Human slavery was part of the fabric of colonial America and the new nation created by the American Revolution. Though the Declaration of Independence states that "all men are created equal," the equality the country's founding fathers had in mind excluded slaves (and women too). One of the stated goals of the First Continental Congress that met in Philadelphia in 1774 was to discontinue the slave trade, but that goal was not achieved.

In 1787 the framers of the U.S. Constitution—many of them slave owners—wrote slavery into law on the assumption that slaves were property, declaring that, for purposes of taxation and representation, each slave would count as three-fifths of a person. In the words of the historian John Hope Franklin, "the Constitution had given recognition to the institution of human slavery, and it was to take seventy-five years to undo that which was accomplished in Philadelphia in 1787."

By 1820 the issue of slavery was a major source of tension between the North and the South. Northern states had passed laws prohibiting slavery, but slavery, a source of cheap labor in the agricultural South, thrived and expanded there. As the United States grew westward and new territories were added, disputes arose about whether or not slavery should be allowed in the new states seeking admission to the Union. Many northerners opposed admitting states that permitted slavery, while southerners supported the expansion of slavery since new slave states would strengthen the pro-slavery bloc in Congress.

For a while, Congress was able to maintain a balance between North and South by keeping the number of free and slave states equal. For each state that was admitted as a slave state, another was admitted as a free state. However, sectional tensions continued to increase until the election of Abraham Lincoln as president in 1860 drove 11 southern states to secede from the Union. Their claim to be an independent nation—the Confederate States of America—led to the Civil War (1861–1865).

The subsequent northern victory left the South's economy and major cities, like Atlanta and Richmond, in ruins. For 12 years following the war—the period known as Reconstruction—northern troops who occupied the South tried to enforce laws guaranteeing equality for blacks. Under northern pressure and supervision blacks were permitted to vote, and some were even elected to Congress. From 1869 to 1877, when Reconstruction ended, 14 blacks served at one time or another in the U.S. House of Representatives. Hiram Revels and Blanche Bruce, both from Mississippi, served in the U.S. Senate. Some northern congressmen called for a redistribution of slaveholders' land as compensation to former slaves for their years in bondage. Thaddeus Stevens of Pennsylvania wanted every ex-slave to have "forty acres and a mule."

However, when the federal government failed to overcome southern white resistance, it lost interest in recreating a new southern society built on racial justice. Reconstruction ended when the last federal troops were pulled out of the South in 1877. The southern white power structure quickly found ways to subordinate and intimidate the former slaves. Whites wrote new laws to keep blacks from voting. These included having to pay to vote (poll tax) and having to read a difficult passage from the state constitution to the satisfaction of the white registrar (literacy test). By the 1890s these requirements had disenfranchised all but a few blacks.

To separate the races and keep blacks in their place, southerners constructed a vast network of local "Jim Crow" laws and practices. Jim Crow was a black minstrel caricature made popular by a song in the 1830s. By mid-century the name *Jim Crow* became a common term for blacks. By 1900 the name described the system of institutionalized segregation that governed almost every aspect of life in the South.

Throughout the South signs reading "White" and "Colored" designated separate public facilities for each race—drinking fountains, restrooms, theaters, bus and train stations. Social custom also defined the relationship between the races. Blacks had to tip their hats and step aside when whites came by, while whites were not expected to remove their hats even when they entered a black home. Black people had to address white people as Mr. and Mrs. and Miss and call them "Sir" and "Ma'am," while white people called blacks by their first names. A black person could be arrested—or even lynched—for talking back to a white person. In South Carolina black and white cotton-mill workers weren't even allowed to look out the same window.

Black children were exposed to segregation early. They were excluded from libraries, parks and pools, and they were not allowed to attend school with white children. Schools for blacks were ramshackle cabins and shacks that were small, overcrowded and unheated. What books and equipment they had were often castoffs from white schools, except in the state of Florida, which had separate "white" and "Negro" textbooks.

This total separation of the races that pervaded the South by the end of the nineteenth century was legalized at the highest level of government in 1896 when the U.S. Supreme Court rendered its decision in the *Plessy v. Ferguson* case. In 1892, Homer Plessy brought suit against a Louisiana railroad company that refused to let him sit in a whites-only car. Plessy looked white, but he was known to have had a black great-grandmother. After he bought a train ticket from New Orleans to a town near the state line, he entered the train and sat down in a car reserved for whites. When he refused to move to the car for blacks, the police arrested him and removed him from the train.

He sued the railroad, arguing that segregation was illegal under the Fourteenth Amendment, an amendment added to the Constitution in 1868 to provide equal protection to newly freed slaves. When Plessy's case went all the way to the Supreme Court, the Court ruled against him. The Supreme Court argued that segregation on the railroad was constitutional as long as "separate but equal" facilities were available to blacks and whites. The decision established the separate-but-equal doctrine that was to serve as the legal foundation of the vast network of Jim Crow laws that maintained segregation throughout the South.

While most former slaves tried to survive as best they could in the South, others went north to look for work and a better life. However, jobs in the North were hard to come by and racism was rampant there as well.

Marcus Garvey, who came to New York by way of Jamaica, Central America and London, founded the Universal Negro Improvement Association (UNIA) in 1914 "to promote the spirit of race pride" after he concluded there was little hope for black people in America. His goal was to foster worldwide unity among black people and establish an understanding of the greatness of African culture. Convinced that blacks could not establish their identity or secure their rights in countries where they were a minority, Garvey urged blacks to stop trying to integrate themselves into white society. He advocated a "back to Africa" movement in the hope that an independent black nation could be established in Africa. Garvey's popularity among American blacks ended in 1925 after he was convicted of mail fraud and sent to prison.

Meanwhile, blacks in the North pressed for better working conditions. In 1917, 10,000 blacks marched down Fifth Avenue in New York City to protest racial discrimination, while in the 1920s Chicago blacks staged a "Jobs For Negroes" campaign. In Harlem, blacks demonstrated and won the right to be hired at white-owned businesses and local utility companies.

Even in the South urban blacks found ways to protest against the way they were treated. By the end of the nineteenth century blacks had boycotted segregated streetcar lines in more than 25 cities. In Montgomery, Alabama, a two-year black boycott of the city's Jim Crow car lines caused local transportation companies to give in to the boycotters' demands before new city ordinances restored segregated seating.

In 1939 a historic event took place in Washington, D.C. that anticipated the later civil rights movement. On Easter Sunday the black soprano Marian Anderson gave an outdoor concert at the Lincoln Memorial after she was denied the use of Constitution Hall because of her race.

Raised in south Philadelphia, Anderson had established an international reputation in Europe. In 1938 Howard University in Washington had requested a concert by Marian Anderson. When her agent, Sol Hurok, tried to reserve Constitution Hall, the largest concert hall in the nation's capital, for April 9, 1939, he was told the date was taken. When Hurok suggested other dates, he was told these dates were also taken. The hall was owned by the Daughters of the American Revolution (DAR), whose ancestors fought against the British in the American Revolution. It was soon learned that the DAR had a clause in its lease that prohibited blacks from performing in the hall.

When the news got out, many were shocked. Public officials, religious leaders, writers and private citizens from different walks of life protested. Leading musicians canceled their concerts at Constitution Hall, including the famous violinist, Jascha Heifetz, who said he would be ashamed to perform there.

The most dramatic protest came from Eleanor Roosevelt, who was a member of the DAR. When she announced her resignation from the DAR in her nationally syndicated newspaper column, "My Day," her action made headlines in newspapers all across the country. Other DAR members and even some local chapters protested the policy of their national body in Washington.

Hurok finally was able to announce that Marian Anderson was going to sing in Washington after all, but not at Constitution Hall. The Department of the Interior of the federal government invited Miss Anderson to sing at an outdoor concert at the Lincoln Memorial on Easter Sunday. On Easter morning 1939, 75,000 people—men, women, children, black and white—gathered for the concert. Those with special invitations who sat on the platform included Supreme Court Justice Hugo Black, Secretary of the Treasury Henry Morgenthau, and at least a dozen members of Congress. After Secretary of the Interior Harold Ickes introduced Marian Anderson to the crowd, she opened her historic concert by singing the national anthem, with the majestic statue of Abraham Lincoln behind her. Then she sang "America," "Ave Maria," an aria and three spirituals.

That Easter concert and the name of Marian Anderson would be forever linked in the minds and memories of a generation of Americans. The concert proved that no matter how much racism there was in America there was also a heartfelt longing on the part of many of its citizens for a more just and tolerant society.

World War II proved to be an important watershed for black Americans. At home black workers held meetings to protest discrimination in the national defense effort, while many more enlisted in the military. Of the 16 million Americans who served in the armed forces, more than one million of them were black. Although black servicemen and women served in segregated units, many of them returned to America from the fight against Nazi racism with dreams of a better life back home. In expressing an opinion shared by many, James Hicks, a black officer, said, "I think there was extreme resentment among black veterans when they came back because they felt, `I paid my dues over there and I'm not going to take this anymore over here.'"

At home the war years saw the emergence of a new civil rights organization. In 1942 James Farmer founded the Congress of Racial Equality (CORE) in Chicago to fight against discrimination using the techniques of nonviolent protest and passive resistance that Mohandas Gandhi used against the British in India. Farmer was the son of a college professor in Texas who had been the first black American to earn a doctoral degree. After receiving a divinity degree from Howard University, Farmer went to Chicago to do further graduate work at the University of Chicago. While he was working for the Fellowship of Reconciliation (FOR), he started CORE.

CORE pioneered the sit-in, which it used to integrate a restaurant and roller-skating rink in Chicago. By 1944 CORE had chapters in five other American cities—New York, Los Angeles, Detroit, Philadelphia and Pittsburgh. In 1947 CORE and its sister organization, FOR, organized the first "freedom ride." A racially mixed group of nine riders traveled by bus through the upper South on what CORE called the "Journey of Reconciliation."

The purpose of the journey was to test segregation policies on interstate bus lines following the decision of the Supreme Court in 1946 that declared segregated seating of interstate passengers unconstitutional. However, the ride only went to show how segregated bus travel really was in the South. In North Carolina some of the black riders were arrested and forced to serve on a chain gang. The man who organized the march on Washington 16 years

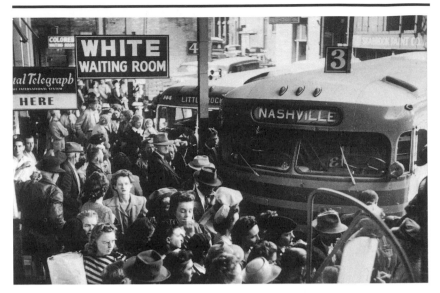

People boarding a bus at a segregated bus station in Memphis, Tennessee in 1943. *(Library of Congress)*

later, Bayard Rustin, served 22 days at hard labor for his part in the ride.

In 1947 Jackie Robinson became the first black player in major league baseball when he was brought up to play for the Brooklyn Dodgers. Robinson was taunted and threatened many times, but resistance against him gradually died down after he proved his worth. In 1949 he won the National League batting crown, hitting .342, and was named the league's most valuable player.

In 1948 President Harry Truman issued a directive calling for an end to segregation in the armed forces.

However, despite these modest postwar gains, blacks continued to be denied the basic rights of citizenship that white people took for granted. The brutal 1955 murder of 14-year-old Emmett Till in Mississippi—one of the thousands of lynchings and unpunished murders in the South of blacks through the years—was proof enough of that. In America blacks were second-class citizens deprived of their most fundamental civil rights—by law in the South, by custom in the North.

CHAPTER ONE NOTES

page 1   "the Constitution had given . . . in 1787." *John Hope Franklin and Alfred A. Moss, Jr.*, **From Slavery to Freedom: A History of African Americans** (6th ed.). New York: Knopf, 1988, p. 78.

page 4   "to promote the spirit of race pride," *William H. Harris and Judith S. Levey (eds.)*, **The New Columbia Encyclopedia**. New York: Columbia University Press, 1975, p. 1048.

page 6   "I think there was . . . over here.'" *Henry Hampton and Steve Fayer*, **Voices of Freedom: An Oral History of the Civil Rights Movement from the 1950s through the 1980s**. New York: Bantam, 1990, p. xxiv.

CHAPTER **Two**

SEPARATE AND UNEQUAL
School Desegregation Court Cases

The first legal challenges to have any significant effect on segregation were those made by the National Association for the Advancement of Colored People (NAACP)—the oldest civil rights organization in the country.

The NAACP was formed after a 1908 lynching of two blacks in Springfield, Illinois led to a call by Mary Ovington, a white woman, for a conference to discuss ways to achieve political and social equality for blacks. The conference led to the founding of the NAACP the following year. As one of the organization's founders, W.E.B. Du Bois, noted, "The NAACP started with a lynching 100 years after the birth of Abraham Lincoln, and in the city of Springfield, Illinois which was his longtime residence."

The new biracial organization committed itself to eliminating racial discrimination and segregation in all areas of American life by peaceful and lawful means. Eight prominent Americans—seven whites and a black—served on the original board of the NAACP. The single black board member was Du Bois, who rejected the gradualism of Booker T. Washington and demanded immediate equality for blacks. He edited the NAACP magazine, *The Crisis*, which reported on race relations around the world.

The NAACP grew so rapidly that in 1915 it was able to organize a partial boycott of the film *The Birth of a Nation*, which portrayed blacks of the Reconstruction era in an insulting way. Most of the NAACP's early efforts were directed against lynchings. Partially as a result of the organization's efforts, the number of lynchings decreased and the practice virtually disappeared by the 1950s.

In the 1930s the NAACP embarked on a campaign to contest segregation in American education through legal challenges in the courts. The strategy was based on a report by Nathan Margold, a white lawyer for the NAACP who advocated challenging the constitutionality of the separate but equal doctrine enshrined in the 1896 *Plessy v. Ferguson* decision of the Supreme Court. Margold recommended targeting the *Plessy* decision, which he contended was vulnerable because it was badly written, poorly thought out and based on legal cases that preceded the Civil War and the Fourteenth Amendment.

In 1935 the director of the NAACP convinced Charles Houston, the organization's chief legal counsel, to take a leave of absence from Howard University to lead the NAACP legal campaign. Houston's was a brilliant legal mind. The only child of an educated middle-class Washington couple, he had graduated with honors from Amherst College (the only black student in the class of 1915) and served as an army officer in World War I. After earning both his law degree and doctorate from Harvard Law School, Houston returned to Washington where he worked in his father's law firm and taught law at Howard.

In 1929 after he was appointed vice-dean of the law school, he set out to improve the school's program. He upgraded entrance requirements, extended the academic year, closed the night school and hired well-respected legal scholars as guest lecturers. Within two years Howard Law School received full accreditation from the American Bar Association (ABA) and joined the Association of American Law Schools.

Using the Margold report, Houston forged his own legal strategy to attack segregation. His plan was to begin at the highest educational level—graduate and professional schools—and then work down through the university and college, high school and finally elementary school levels. At the highest level of education the injustice was most obvious and the prospect of change least threatening. At the elementary, secondary and even university levels separate white and black schools were available, but for the few blacks who continued beyond college most states did not provide separate law schools, medical schools or other graduate-school programs.

Houston decided to start with law schools since the judges hearing the cases were familiar with them. As law school graduates themselves, the judges would recognize the folly of having separate law schools, especially for one or a few black law students.

In 1935 Houston learned about a young black man, Donald Murray, who was denied admission to the all-white law school of the University of Maryland. Houston and Thurgood Marshall, his former student then practicing law in Baltimore, argued Murray's case in Baltimore city court. Houston's argument was simple: A black citizen of Maryland should have the right to study law at the state university since there were no black law schools in the state.

Southern states sometimes circumvented the problem by giving the black student a scholarship to study in another state rather than admit the student to a state institution. Houston and Marshall argued that since Murray wanted to practice law in Maryland, offering him an out-of-state legal education would violate the principle of equal treatment under the separate-but-equal doctrine of existing law. The presiding judge agreed with them. He ordered the University of Maryland law school to admit Murray. The state appealed the case, but a higher court upheld the ruling. By forcing the University of Maryland law school to integrate, the NAACP won its first important legal victory against segregation.

In 1936 Houston went to Missouri to argue another law school case. Lloyd Gaines, a 25-year-old black man, was denied admission to the all-white University of Missouri law school. The state promised to build a law school on the campus of Lincoln University, a black school, if Gaines would apply there, or if he was not prepared to wait several years for the facility to be constructed, the state agreed to pay his tuition at a law school in another state. When Gaines lost his case at the circuit court level, Houston appealed the decision to the U.S. Supreme Court.

Two and a half years later, on November 9, 1938, Houston argued the case before the Supreme Court and won. The Supreme

Court ruled that Gaines was entitled to attend the University of Missouri School of Law. The nation's highest court declared that states had an obligation to provide equal education to all their citizens and ruled that states could not send their black students out of state instead of educating them inside the state nor could they ask black students to wait while they built separate schools for them in the state. The ruling had important implications: If states had to provide equal legal education for blacks, did not they also have to provide equal education at the college, high school and elementary school levels?

Thurgood Marshall, who succeeded Houston as chief legal counsel of the NAACP (and became the first black member of the Supreme Court in 1967), established the NAACP Legal Defense Fund in order to challenge more segregated graduate schools. Marshall pursued two cases, involving black graduate school applicants in Texas and Oklahoma, all the way to the Supreme Court. In 1950 the Court ruled in favor of the NAACP in both cases, declaring that separate education for blacks that was not truly equal was unconstitutional. However, since the Supreme Court ruled that its decision applied only to graduate schools, the separate-but-equal doctrine of *Plessy v. Ferguson* remained intact everywhere else. When federal court rulings began suggesting that segregated schools were bound to be inferior, the NAACP decided the time was ripe not just to insist that black schools be equal to white schools, but to challenge the very constitutionality of the separate-but-equal doctrine of segregation in American education as well.

At a conference in New York in 1950, NAACP lawyers and officials decided to attack segregation on two fronts. They would challenge *Plessy v. Ferguson* directly by arguing that the separate-but-equal doctrine was unconstitutional under the Fourteenth Amendment. However, in case that strategy didn't work, they would argue that under the separate-but-equal doctrine schools should be truly equal and the only way to make them equal was to integrate them. To collect evidence of the psychological damage done to black students as well as the educational deprivation that resulted from segregated schooling, the NAACP called on its offices around the country to gather cases that could be used as part of a broad-based legal attack on segregation.

Thurgood Marshall joined the legal staff of the NAACP in 1936. He argued the landmark 1954 desegregation in education case, *Brown v. Board of Education of Topeka*, before the Supreme Court. In 1967, President Lyndon Johnson appointed him the first black justice on the nation's highest court. *(Library of Congress)*

In 1950 the NAACP Legal Defense Fund filed its first legal challenge to segregation at the elementary school level in South Carolina. In the 1930s Charles Houston had gone to South Carolina with a 16-mm camera to illustrate the injustice of segregated schools. He documented buildings, teachers and pupils in both black and white schools to gather evidence of the huge disparity between the unheated shacks and cabins black children attended and the brick and stone buildings where white children were educated. In 1930 South Carolina spent 10 times more money educating a white child than a black child. Little was changed 20 years later; segregated schools were "separate" but hardly "equal."

At the time of the NAACP's 1950 suit against the school board of Clarendon County, South Carolina (called the *Briggs* case) white students in the county were receiving 60% of the education funds even though there were three times more black students in the county. The organization enlisted the help of black psychologist Kenneth Clark, who had studied the harmful effects of segregated schooling on young blacks. However, his data did not convince the federal district court, which ruled 2-1 against the black parents who brought the suit. Thurgood Marshall and the NAACP appealed the decision to the Supreme Court, but they had to wait almost two years for the court to hear the appeal.

The next NAACP case involved a seven-year-old girl, Linda Brown, who lived in Topeka, Kansas. She had to take a bus to the other side of town to attend an all-black school even though there was a white school close to her house. In its *Brown v. Board of Education of Topeka* suit, NAACP lawyers called expert witnesses to testify about the psychological effects of segregation on black children. The judge dismissed the suit on the grounds that no laws had been violated, though in his ruling he did concede that segregation was harmful to black children.

NAACP suits in other parts of the country also made their way through the appeals process. In June 1952 the Supreme Court announced that it would hear *Briggs v. Clarendon County* and *Brown v. Board of Education of Topeka* in its fall term and then added three more similar cases. The Supreme Court consolidated the five segregation cases under the name of the first case it decided to hear—*Brown v. Board of Education of Topeka*.

On December 9, 1952, spectators packed the Supreme Court and lined the corridors seeking admission to what was to be one of the most important court cases in American history. After six days of arguments the Court convened to decide the case, but it postponed a decision for more than a year. When Chief Justice Fred Vinson died in 1953, President Eisenhower appointed former governor of California Earl Warren to replace him.

On Monday, May 17, 1954, the Supreme Court finally handed down its decision. The Court ruled in favor of the black plaintiffs, declaring that segregation had a detrimental effect on black children because it "generates a feeling of inferiority as to their status in the community that may affect their hearts and minds in a way unlikely ever to be undone." The Court ruling was read by Chief Justice Warren: "We conclude, unanimously, that in the field of public education the doctrine of 'separate but equal' has no place. Separate educational facilities are inherently unequal."

Although the full impact of the landmark decision would not be felt for years, it was the most important civil rights court case in the twentieth century. The ruling reversed the racist separate-but-equal doctrine established by the 1896 *Plessy v. Ferguson* Supreme Court decision and laid the groundwork for the future integration of the segregated school systems of the South.

CHAPTER TWO NOTES

page 9   "The NAACP started . . . longtime residence." Quoted in *Rhoda Lois Blumberg*, **Civil Rights: The 1960s Freedom Struggle** (rev. ed.). Boston: G.K. Hall, 1991, p. 22.

page 15   "generates a feeling . . . to be undone." Quoted in **Civil Rights**, p. 37.

page 15   "We conclude, unanimously . . . unequal." Quoted in *Juan Williams*, **Eyes on the Prize; America's Civil Rights Years 1954–1965**. New York: Penguin, 1988, p. 34.

CHAPTER Three

OPENING BATTLES
Montgomery and Little Rock

On December 1, 1955, Rosa Parks, a 43-year-old seamstress who worked in a department store in downtown Montgomery, Alabama, boarded a bus to go home. She sat down next to a black man in the aisle seat in the first row of the middle section where blacks were allowed to sit when whites didn't need the seats. Two black women were sitting in the same row across the aisle.

City buses throughout the South—where segregation laws reserved seats in front for whites and required blacks to sit in back—had long been the sites of some of the most demeaning scenes of segregation in action. In Montgomery (where more than three-quarters of the passengers were black) and most other southern cities, blacks were not even allowed to walk through the white section to get to the back. After they paid their fare up front, they had to leave the bus and reenter it through the back door. If the white section in front filled up and a white passenger needed a seat, all the black passengers in the row had to stand up and move to the back so the white person could sit down.

It was up to the driver to determine the line between the seats for whites in front and the seats for blacks in back. As more whites got on the bus, the driver told blacks to get up and move back.

On this particular ride Rosa Parks didn't particularly notice that more white passengers boarded the bus at the next stops until she noticed the white man standing over her. The white section in front had filled up, and now the white man needed a seat. "All right, you folks,"the driver called out, "I want those seats." That meant all four black people had to stand up since no black was allowed to sit in a seat parallel with a white. The three other blacks obeyed, but Rosa Parks stayed put.

When the bus driver asked her in a threatening voice if she was going to stand up, Parks quietly but firmly said "No." The driver stopped the bus and told her if she didn't get up he was going to have her arrested. When Parks didn't move, he got off and called the police. In a few minutes two policemen arrived in a squad car. They boarded the bus, arrested Parks, and drove her to the city jail where they booked her for breaking the law.

News of the arrest spread quickly. Rosa Parks was a well-liked, familiar figure at church suppers and prayer meetings and was active in the local NAACP. When E.D. Nixon, a Pullman railroad porter who was a leader of the local NAACP, learned of Rosa Parks' arrest, he knew she was the right person to build a case around. After he raised the bond that released her from jail, he asked her if she would help the NAACP challenge the legality of segregation on city buses. Parks talked it over with her husband and mother, then told Nixon, "If you think it is all right, I'll go along with you."

When Nixon called Ralph Abernathy, the 29-year-old pastor of the First Baptist Church, to inform him of the arrest, Abernathy agreed to help. Nixon invited 18 other ministers to a meeting that evening to discuss the arrest and decide what to do.

In the meantime, when Jo Ann Robinson, an English professor at the all-black Alabama State College, and the other members of the Women's Political Council, who had also talked about staging a bus boycott in Montgomery learned about Rosa Parks' arrest, they decided it was time for the boycott. Robinson drove to her college and stayed up all night mimeographing flyers that called for a one-day bus boycott. In the morning Robinson took the flyers—all 35,000 of them—to the city's black schools. Students she contacted distributed them to the rest of the children, who took them home to their parents.

"Another Negro woman has been arrested and thrown into jail because she refused to get up out of her seat on the bus for a white person to sit down," read the flyer. "This has to be stopped . . . If we do not do something to stop these arrests, they will continue. The next time it may be you, or your daughter, or mother. This woman's case will come up on Monday. We are, therefore, asking every Negro to stay off the buses Monday in protest of the arrest and trial. Don't ride buses to work, to town, to school, and anywhere on Monday."

By the time the ministers met on Friday night, word of the boycott had spread throughout the black community. The ministers at the meeting were split about holding a boycott. About half the ministers left the meeting before it was over, but the remaining half supported the one-day boycott and agreed to pass the word to their congregations on Sunday. When the *Montgomery Advertiser*, the city's largest newspaper, ran a story about the planned boycott on the front page of its Sunday edition, word of the boycott spread to the city's whites and blacks who had not yet heard about it.

The boycott was successful beyond anything the organizers could have hoped for. On Monday the buses were virtually empty and the taxis full because Montgomery's black-owned taxi companies agreed to transport blacks that day for the price of a bus ride—10 cents. In the meantime, in court on that Monday morning Rosa Parks was found guilty of breaking segregation laws and given a suspended sentence.

That afternoon at a meeting of the ministers and other black leaders who supported the boycott, the group decided to call themselves the Montgomery Improvement Association. When it came time to elect a president, many said it was time for new leadership. For months Ralph Abernathy had been trying to get the new pastor of the Dexter Avenue Baptist Church, the Reverend Martin Luther King, Jr., a 26-year-old minister with a doctorate in theology, more involved in community affairs, but he continued to say he was too busy with his duties at his new church.

Rufus Lewis, a community leader who was a member of King's church and knew him to be a very good speaker, nominated him. Nixon liked the idea, seeing King's youth and lack of experience with the city's established black leaders as an advantage. The group elected King their new leader. When King said he wanted to think it over before he accepted, Nixon cut him short. "You ain't got much time to think, 'cause you in the chair from

The 1955–1956 Montomery, Alabama bus boycott thrust Martin Luther King, Jr. into the national spotlight, where he remained until his assassination in 1968. *(Photograph and Prints Division/Schomburg Center for Research in Black Culture–New York Public Library/Astor, Lenox and Tilden Foundations)*

now on." King agreed. "Somebody has to do it," he said, "and if you think I can, I will serve."

That evening a mass meeting was held at the Holt Street Baptist Church. The large church was packed, with cars and people jamming the streets for blocks around the building. Even before the meeting began the hundreds of people who couldn't get inside the church were standing in the street listening to what was going on inside with the help of loudspeakers that had been hooked up on the outside of the building. "They were on fire for freedom," reported the white reporter who covered the meeting for the *Montgomery Advertiser*. "There was a spirit there that no one could capture again . . . it was so powerful."

Martin Luther King, Jr. had little time to prepare his speech. When he was introduced to the crowd, most people had never heard of him. "We are here this evening," he told them, "to say to those who have mistreated us so long that we are tired—tired of being segregated and humiliated; tired of being kicked about by the brutal feet of oppression . . . One of the great glories of democracy is the right to protest for right . . . if you will protest courageously and yet with dignity and Christian love, when the history books are written in future generations the historians will pause and say, `There lived a great people—a black people—who injected new meaning and dignity into the veins of civilization.' That is our challenge and our overwhelming responsibility."

When Rosa Parks was introduced, she was given a standing ovation. Then Reverend Abernathy read the three demands the Montgomery Improvement Association had drafted at its earlier meeting: (1) courteous treatment on buses; (2) seating on a first-come, first-serve basis with whites continuing to sit in front and blacks in back; and (3) hiring of black drivers on black bus routes.

When Abernathy asked those who were in favor of the demands to stand up, nobody moved. Then in ones and twos people rose until soon everybody was standing. Abernathy later said that the fear that had gripped them for so many years suddenly left them that night in the church.

The boycott continued. On Thursday—the fourth day of the boycott—the leaders of the Montgomery Improvement Association (MIA) met with the city commissioners and bus company officials to discuss their demands. They made it clear they were not trying to end segregation. They just wanted respect and open seating in the middle of buses, which was the practice in other Alabama cities, including Mobile, whose buses were owned by the same bus company.

The city and the bus company refused to budge, so the boycott continued. To break the boycott the city threatened to fine black taxi drivers if they didn't charge every passenger the minimum 45-cent fare. The boycott leaders feared they might lose the taxis as their main source of alternate travel for blacks who refused to ride the buses.

King called Reverend Jemison, who had led a successful bus boycott in Baton Rouge, Louisiana two years earlier. In 1953 the black community in Baton Rouge had succeeded in persuading the city council to pass an ordinance that improved the situation for blacks on city buses. Blacks still sat in back and whites in front, but the ordinance allowed blacks to sit in empty seats in the middle of the bus on a first-come, first-serve basis.

When the white bus drivers ignored the ordinance and continued saving the seats in the middle for whites and making blacks give up their seats in that section when whites wanted to sit down, the city's blacks staged a one-day bus boycott. However, the state attorney general intervened in the dispute and declared the city ordinance illegal. Three months later when the blacks of Baton Rouge staged another bus boycott, city officials agreed to a variation of the nullified ordinance that reserved the seats in front for whites and the long seat in back for blacks, but allowed all the seats in between to be filled on a first-come, first-serve basis.

Jemison told King about the car pool system they used during the second boycott (which lasted a week) and suggested the Montgomery boycott people organize a similar plan, complete with pick-up and drop-off points and a communications system connecting those who needed rides with those offering them.

For the next mass meeting at the church more than 150 people who owned cars volunteered, and the MIA immediately set up a transportation committee to work out the details of a car pool system. Within one week a system was fully operational with 90 pick-up and drop-off stations around the city.

The mass meetings that MIA held twice a week—on Monday and Thursday nights—kept up morale and raised money to pay for the boycott. Financial support also came from sympathetic blacks and whites in the North as well as other parts of the South. These donations, which came from as far away as Tokyo and Singapore, allowed the MIA to purchase a fleet of 15 new station wagons to transport the boycotters. Each station wagon was registered as the property of a different church with the name of the church written on it, which is why they were called "rolling churches."

As both sides dug in for the long battle, Martin Luther King, Jr. continually emphasized the importance of nonviolence for the struggle to succeed. He told his audiences they needed to win the support of compassionate and fair-minded people by meeting provocations and threats with love rather than anger. King and the other MIA leaders knew that it was essential for their success that they win public support by seizing the moral high ground. Nonviolence was their greatest weapon. The tone of the bus boycott and the civil rights movement that flowed from it was set in these critical months.

"One feels history is being made in Montgomery these days," wrote a white librarian in a letter to a Montgomery newspaper. "It is hard to imagine a soul so dead, a heart so hard, a vision so blinded and provincial as to not be awed with admiration at the quiet dignity, discipline, and dedication with which the Negroes have conducted the boycott." She compared the movement to Gandhi's nonviolent struggle against the British in India.

With downtown businesses and the bus company suffering mounting financial losses, white efforts to break the boycott intensified. The mayor denounced the MIA leaders as "a group of Negro radicals" and refused to negotiate with them. The segregationists' resolve increased and membership in the racist White Citizens' Council mushroomed. The mayor and other city officials joined the White Citizens' Council to show their support for the hard-line segregationist cause.

As tensions grew, so did the violence. In late January somebody threw a bomb at King's house, but his wife and infant daughter, who were in the back room, escaped injury. When a large crowd of angry blacks gathered in front of his house afterward, King assured them that everything was all right. "I want it to be known through the length and breadth of this land that if I am stopped, this movement will not stop. If I am stopped, our work will not stop. For what we are doing is right. What we are doing is just. And God is with us."

Two days later on February 1—the same day Nixon's home was bombed—Fred Gray, a black lawyer, filed suit challenging the constitutionality of bus segregation on behalf of Rosa Parks and four other women. Since city officials were not going to compromise on the issue, King, Abernathy, Nixon and the other MIA leaders knew they needed a ruling from the U.S. Supreme Court.

To break the boycott, the city's politicians convened a grand jury for the purpose of prosecuting MIA leaders under an old law that prohibited boycotts. On February 21, 1956, the grand jury indicted 89 boycott leaders, including King, Abernathy and 23 other ministers. The following day the city arrested them for committing "conspiracy to conduct an illegal boycott."

Their trial drew national attention, and the publicity created by the trial helped people outside the South learn more about segregation. Most people who read about the boycott could not help but be impressed by the dignity of the boycotters and the reasonableness of their demands. Furthermore, their behavior contrasted sharply with the violence of the racists and the intransigence of city officials. In the months and years ahead this kind of publicity became one of the most effective weapons of the civil rights movement.

King was convicted and fined $1,000, but the conviction only enhanced his moral authority. After his release on bond, he traveled around the country giving speeches to publicize and raise money for the boycott. When the boycott continued through the spring and into summer, a reporter for a national newspaper asked a small, elderly black woman if she was tired of walking. She said, "My feet is tired, but my soul is rested."

In June there was a breakthrough when Rosa Parks and the four other women challenging the constitutionality of bus segregation won their case in federal district court. While the city appealed the decision to the U.S. Supreme Court, the boycott of the city's segregated buses continued.

On November 13, 1956, the mayor got the restraining order he had long been seeking in state court to prevent blacks from waiting on street corners for their rides on the grounds that they were a "public nuisance." However, the decision the U.S. Supreme Court handed down the same day overshadowed his victory. The nation's highest court upheld the decision of the federal district court on behalf of Rosa Parks and the four other women who brought the suit that segregation on buses was unconstitutional. Segregationists challenged the decision on the grounds that it violated states' rights, but the Supreme Court refused to hear their challenge.

The Supreme Court decision sealed the victory of the boycotters by ruling that segregation was just as unconstitutional on Montgomery's city buses as it was in public schools. Once again the nation's highest court dealt a devastating blow to the edifice of legalized segregation, which had been enshrined in law since the separate-but-equal *Plessy v. Ferguson* decision of 1896.

When the written mandate of the Supreme Court arrived in Montgomery shortly before Christmas 1956, boycott leaders marked the occasion by taking a bus ride. Dr. King, Dr. Abernathy, E.D. Nixon and the Reverend Glenn Smiley, a white Southern ally, got on the bus, paid the driver and sat down in front. Their ride on the first integrated bus was without incident.

Although snipers shot at the buses at night and the homes and churches of Abernathy and several other black ministers were bombed, the victory held and inspired blacks to launch bus boycotts in other cities—Birmingham, Mobile and Tallahassee, Florida. "We felt that we were somebody," said Jo Ann Robinson later, "that we had forced the white man to give what we knew was our own citizenship."

One of the most important results of the Montgomery bus boycott for the future of the civil rights movement was the creation of the Southern Christian Leadership Conference (SCLC) by King, Abernathy and black ministers across the South. The organization, which committed itself to work for desegregation and civil rights, elected King as its president.

The Montgomery bus boycott, which showed that black people using nonviolence could confront segregation and win, was a landmark event in the civil rights struggle for several reasons: It mobilized and organized the entire black community of Montgomery with great effectiveness; it introduced nonviolent protest on a mass scale as a successful weapon against segregation; it enlisted the support of others through national press coverage; it sought and received help from the federal bench; and it brought to the fore as a leader the Reverend Martin Luther King, Jr.

*   *   *

Coming in the wake of the Supreme Court's call for the desegregation of southern schools, the court's vindication of the Montgomery bus boycott sent shock waves through the South. White Citizens Councils sprang up, the Ku Klux Klan recruited new members and southern state legislatures passed laws to strengthen segregation. Mississippi amended its constitution so that it could shut down its schools if necessary to avoid desegregation, and the state legislature passed a law that banned potentially troublesome lawsuits by the NAACP. On June 1, 1956—during the Montgomery bus boycott—the Alabama state legislature passed a law that banned the NAACP from operating in the state.

This defiant mood was soon to engulf the relatively progressive state of Arkansas, as became apparent not long after the Little Rock school board became the first school board in the South to announce its intention to comply with the Supreme Court ruling on school desegregation. The board's decision was supported by both of the city's major white-run daily newspapers.

Observers of race relations in the South were not surprised. Arkansas had already shown itself to be more progressive than other southern states. Both the medical and law schools of the University of Arkansas admitted blacks voluntarily before the 1954 Supreme Court ruling declared school segregation unconstitutional, and close to half the students at the University Graduate Center in Little Rock were black. The Little Rock library, parks, and city buses were all integrated, and there were blacks on the police force.

In the summer of 1954, shortly after the *Brown* decision, Little Rock's school superintendent drafted a desegregation plan that called for the integration of two high schools under construction that were scheduled to open in the fall of 1956. The plan also called for the integration of the junior high schools the following year and eventually the city's elementary schools as well.

However, in May of 1955 the Little Rock school board came up with a plan of its own that called for the integration of only one school—Central High School—to take effect in September 1957. Furthermore, under the school board plan only a limited number of black students would be allowed to attend the high school, which had 2,000 white students from working-class families.

Governor Orval Faubus curried favor with the growing white opposition to integration by joining forces with those who wanted to delay and obstruct the school board plan to integrate Central High. Seeking reelection as governor, he discerned which way the political wind was blowing. Citing a poll showing that the vast majority of state residents were against court-ordered school integration, Faubus announced that he would not force acceptance of something that people opposed so overwhelmingly. In the meantime, the state legislature passed new laws to help the state defend segregation, including laws making lawsuits to integrate schools more difficult to file and providing state funds to groups fighting desegregation.

As the time approached for the school board plan to go into effect, the school board did everything it could to limit the number of black students who could attend Central High. It rejected two-thirds of the 75 black students who signed up and tried to dissuade the remaining 25 from attending by telling their parents their children would be at a disadvantage when it came to playing sports or participating in extracurricular activities. As a result of these tactics, only nine black students enrolled at Central High.

Governor Faubus supported a last-minute court suit by a group of white mothers that sought to block the integration of Central High. Then on the day before the opening of school in Little Rock, the governor went on statewide television to announce that he was calling out the Arkansas National Guard to Central High, allegedly to protect lives and property. He warned that if the nine black students tried to attend Central High, "blood would run in the streets."

The next morning—the first day of school—250 Arkansas National Guardsmen stood outside Central High to protect the empty building from a mob that never materialized, while the school board ordered the black students not to attempt to attend Central High "until this dilemma is legally resolved." However, when the federal district judge ordered the board to implement the desegregation plan, the board told the nine black students to report to the school the next day.

On the next morning, the students were supposed to meet at the home of Daisy Bates, president of the state NAACP, so that she could transport them to the high school as a group. But

15-year-old Elizabeth Eckford, whose parents hadn't been informed of the plan because they didn't have a phone, set off for school on her own.

When she got off the bus near the school and began walking toward the front entrance of the high school, an angry crowd approached and followed her down what she later called "the longest block I ever walked in my whole life." When she reached the front entrance, the soldiers didn't let her pass. When she saw one of the soldiers let some white students through, she went over to him, but he blocked her way. "When I tried to squeeze past him, he raised his bayonet, and then the other guards moved in and raised their bayonets." That's when she heard somebody shout, "Lynch her! Lynch her!" She noticed "the face of an old woman, and it seemed a kind face, but when I looked again, she spit on me."

When Eckford went to the bus stop at the end of the block to leave, gangs of jeering, taunting whites followed her. "Drag her over to the tree," one of them shouted. Two white people—a woman whose husband taught at a local black college and the education reporter of the *New York Times*—stayed with her until the bus came, and accompanied her home. For weeks and months afterward Elizabeth Eckford had nightmares that woke her in the middle of the night. The other eight students who were driven to Central as a group were also turned away by the soldiers.

The governor's popularity soared as Arkansas whites praised him for defying the federal court order and keeping troops stationed at the school. When the school board requested that the federal district judge suspend the integration plan, the judge refused. President Eisenhower, who had hoped to remain above the battle, was forced to get involved when the standoff continued. He invited Governor Faubus to his summer home in Newport, Rhode Island to discuss the crisis. After their conversation President Eisenhower was under the impression that the governor understood his responsibility for making sure a lawful federal court order was obeyed.

One week later when the federal judge ordered the governor to remove his troops from the high school, Faubus announced his compliance and then immediately left town for a southern governors' conference in Georgia. There he basked in the favorable publicity that came with standing up to the federal government in the defense of segregation.

On Monday morning, September 23, the nine black students were driven under police guard from Daisy Bates' home to Central High, where they were able to enter a side entrance before a large crowd of whites could react. When the whites found out the students had slipped into the building, they turned on the reporters and photographers who were there to cover the story for the national media. They punched them and smashed their equipment.

By noon several thousand angry whites had collected outside the school. The principal called the nine black students to his office to tell them he was sending them home for their own safety as the police were having trouble controlling the crowd. After the students were escorted out of the school and made it home unharmed, Daisy Bates told reporters that the black students would not return to Central High until President Eisenhower could guarantee their safety.

President Eisenhower called the riot "disgraceful." With Faubus continuing to enjoy the limelight at the southern governors' conference, the mayor of Little Rock was left to deal with the growing crisis. Not sure he had enough police to handle the growing number of segregationists who were coming to Little Rock to block the integration of Central High, the mayor asked the president to consider sending in federal troops to maintain law and order. The next morning when an even bigger mob assembled outside Central High, the mayor called the Justice Department and made a formal request.

Convinced now that Little Rock was an issue of insurrection more than integration, President Eisenhower ordered riot-trained units from the 101st Airborne Division to Little Rock and mobilized the Arkansas National Guard. He told the country on national television that while it saddened him to have to send troops to Little Rock, he was determined not to allow mob rule to override the orders of a federal court.

The next morning the nine black students met once more at the home of Daisy Bates, but this time they were escorted to Central High by heavily armed U.S. paratroopers. When they arrived, hundreds of soldiers with drawn bayonets surrounding the school were keeping the mob back as army helicopters circled

Students leaving a U.S. Army station wagon to attend Central High School in Little Rock in 1957, after President Dwight Eisenhower ordered federal troops to Arkansas to protect them. *(Library of Congress)*

overhead. Inside the school the paratroopers served as body-guards for the black students.

Governor Faubus—now a segregationist hero throughout the South—went on statewide television to complain that Little Rock was "an occupied territory" and that soldiers with bayonets were scaring little girls. After the 101st Airborne troops were withdrawn to an army base outside Little Rock, leaving the Arkansas National Guard at the school, the most rabid segregationist students who had boycotted classes returned, and the atmosphere grew more tense and ugly. Hostile whites threw things at the black students and harassed them with name-calling, shovings, and trippings.

On May 29, 1958, after a long year of animosity and friction, Ernest Green, the only one of the nine black students who was a senior, graduated. At the ceremony every one of the graduating students was applauded as they went up one by one to receive their diploma. Then it was Green's turn. "When they called my name, there was nothing, just the name, and then there was eerie silence. Nobody clapped. But I figured they didn't have to because after I got that diploma, that was it. I had accomplished what I had come there for."

Governor Faubus, who was reelected in a landslide, closed Little Rock's public high schools for the 1958–59 school year rather than let them be integrated. When the Supreme Court ruled that closing the schools was unconstitutional and segregation must not be perpetuated by "evasive schemes," Little Rock reopened its public high schools in the fall of 1959 and integrated them in accordance with federal orders.

The lesson of Little Rock was not lost on southern politicians. Defending segregation and defying the federal government was a sure way to win political popularity. Southern governors and other state politicians became more vocal about the threat from enemies of the "Southern way of life"—civil rights groups, northern politicians, Communist sympathizers and federal courts, especially the Supreme Court.

CHAPTER THREE NOTES

page 18   "If you think . . . with you." *David J. Garrow,* **Bearing the Cross: Martin Luther King, Jr., and the Southern Christian Leadership Conference**. New York: Vintage, 1988, p. 14.

pages 18–19 "Another Negro woman . . . on Monday." **Bearing**, pp. 16–17.

pages 19–20 "You ain't got much time . . . I will serve." *Stephen B. Oates,* **Let the Trumpet Sound: A Life of Martin Luther King, Jr.** New York: Harper & Row, 1982, p. 68.

page 21   "They were on fire . . . so powerful." *Beatrice Siegel,* **The Year They Walked: Rosa Parks and the Montgomery Bus Boycott**. New York: Four Winds Press, 1992, p. 48.

page 21   "We are here . . . responsibility." Quoted in **Eyes**, p. 76.

page 23   "One feels history . . . conducted the boycott." Quoted in **Eyes**, p. 79.

page 23   "I want it to be known . . . with us." *Taylor Branch*, **Parting the Waters: America in the King Years, 1954–1963.** New York: Simon & Schuster, 1988, p. 166.

page 24   "My feet is tired, but my soul is rested." *Janet Harris*, **The Long Freedom Road**. New York: McGraw-Hill, 1967, p. 43.

page 25   "We felt that we were . . . citizenship." **Year**, p. 84.

page 27   "blood would run in the streets." **Civil Rights**, p. 60.

page 28   "the longest block . . . When I tried to squeeze . . . Lynch her! . . . the face of an old woman . . . Drag her over to the tree." **Eyes**, pp. 101–102.

page 30–31 "When they called . . . there for." **Voices**, pp. 51–52.

Four

BOLD NEW CHALLENGES TO SEGREGATION

Student Sit-ins and Freedom Rides

The events of the 1950s—the *Brown v. Board of Education of Topeka* Supreme Court decision, the Montgomery bus boycott, the show of federal force in Little Rock—all made a deep impression on a new generation of young blacks. Civil rights organizations tried as best they could to focus their energy and idealism. The NAACP opened more Youth Council chapters around the country, and the newer SCLC welcomed growing numbers of young black people interested in participating in the civil rights struggle. The success of the broad-based, nonviolent Montgomery bus boycott galvanized many blacks, young and old, and set the stage for the new forms of resistance that sprang up all over the South in the early 1960s.

A new important chapter in the civil rights movement began on the afternoon of February 1, 1960, when four black students from North Carolina Agricultural and Technical College in Greensboro, North Carolina went to the segregated lunch counter at Woolworth's and ordered coffee. When they were refused service, they stayed there until the store closed. The following week the Greensboro students staged more sit-ins.

Protesters in front of an F.W. Woolworth Co. store in New York City, demonstrating against the store's segregationist policy in the South. *(Photographs and prints Division/Schomburg Center for Research in Black Culture–New York Public Library/Astor, Lenox and Tilden Foundations)*

As news of that first Greensboro sit-in spread, sit-ins sprang up in other cities. By the middle of February sit-ins had spread to 11 southern cities. Students in the North staged demonstrations at national chain stores like Woolworth's that practiced segregation in their southern stores. Unlike Montgomery or Little Rock or even the freedom rides, the student protests were national in scope.

One of the most sustained and successful student sit-in campaigns took place in Nashville, Tennessee. There a group called the Nashville Student Movement launched a major challenge to segregation in the city. The students who organized the group had taken workshops in nonviolence given by James Lawson, a young black minister who was the southern field secretary of the Fellowship of Reconciliation (FOR), an interracial pacifist group committed to the principles of nonviolent resistance. FOR had sent

Lawson to Nashville to give workshops in nonviolence there and in other southern cities while he studied theology at Vanderbilt.

Lawson became an important influence on the new generation of black student activists eager to confront racism, and his deep commitment to nonviolence did much to set the tone and direction of students who joined the civil rights movement. In the 1950s Lawson had chosen to go to prison rather than serve in the military during the Korean War. After he was paroled from prison, he was placed in the care of Methodist ministers. They sent him to India for three years as a missionary. There he studied the nonviolent philosophy of Mohandas Gandhi.

Upon his return to the United States, he resumed his studies at the Oberlin College School of Theology in Ohio. When he learned about the Montgomery bus boycott, he went to Alabama to meet with the Reverend Martin Luther King, Jr. Lawson impressed King with his explanation of Gandhi's belief in nonviolent resistance as the most effective way to achieve social change. King encouraged Lawson to spread the ideals of Gandhian nonviolence throughout the civil rights movement.

In his Nashville workshops Lawson taught the discipline of nonviolence to students who wanted to challenge segregation. He trained them to sit quietly while he had other students, playing the role of segregationists, curse, jeer, jab and spit at them. Diane Nash and John Lewis, who later became national leaders of the civil rights movement, were two of the Nashville students who enrolled in the workshops. Nash, a Fisk University student from Chicago, didn't like the segregation she found in Nashville. She went to the Tuesday night workshops where the participants learned the philosophy and tactics of nonviolence and how to protect their heads from injury and how to protect each other from severe beatings. John Lewis, a student at the American Baptist Theological Seminary in Nashville, said the workshops they attended became the most important things in their lives.

The Nashville Student Movement that Nash, Lewis and others who took the nonviolence workshops had organized made plans to begin their challenge to segregation in Nashville with department store lunch counters. Their idea was to send students to a lunch counter to try to order something. If they were arrested, other students would take their place. When they succeeded in integrating one lunch counter, they would go on to others. After the lunch counters, they planned on targeting Nashville's segregated libraries and movie theaters.

"When the Greensboro students sat in on February 1," said Diane Nash, "we simply made plans to join their effort by sitting in at the same chains. We were surprised and delighted to hear reports of other cities joining in the sit-ins. We started feeling the power of the idea whose time had come." The Nashville Student Movement mobilized 200 people for sit-ins at the city's major stores.

At the first Nashville sit-in the waitresses were as nervous as the students. "They must have dropped $2,000 worth of dishes that day," recalled Nash. "We were sitting there trying not to laugh but at the same time were were scared to death." She remembered sitting in class with sweating palms before having to go to a demonstration in the afternoon. "I was really afraid," she said.

On Saturday, February 27, at one of the stores a large group of young whites pulled the students off the lunch-counter seats and beat them. The police arrested the protesters for "disorderly conduct," but that did not stop the demonstration. As soon as the police marched the students off to the wagons, a second wave of students sat in at the lunch counter. Then there was a third wave. Nash observed that no matter how many they arrested, there always seemed to be another group of students to take their place.

The arrests did not deter the Nashville students from continuing their sit-ins. On March 2 when they sat in at the city Greyhound and Trailways bus terminals, police arrested 63 of them. Two weeks later the first sit-in victory in the country took place when four students, after being severely beaten, were finally served at the Greyhound terminal. The next day two unexploded bombs were found in that same terminal.

The sit-ins hurt store business in Nashville. Whites were afraid to go downtown and blacks withheld their business from the stores where the sit-ins were taking place. Business owners proposed a 90-day truce during which they would serve blacks in part of the lunchroom or restaurant where whites were served, but the students refused the offer since the proposed plan still limited black access to lunchrooms and restaurants.

The spontaneous student sit-ins in southern cities in the spring of 1960 demonstrated the dissatisfaction of young blacks with segregation and their determination to change it. In fact, some observers of the civil rights movement point to the first Greensboro sit-in, not the Montgomery bus boycott, as the real turning point in the history of the civil rights movement. "Montgomery was a reaction; Greensboro was an act," wrote the social historian Lerone Bennett, Jr. "The students knew what they were about: they did not stumble into it."

The student sit-ins also signaled a shift away from the older, more established civil rights groups, like the NAACP, which believed the best chance for effective change came through the courts and through legislation in Congress. Journalist Louis Lomax wrote that the sit-ins were evidence of an important change in the battle against segregation away from the courtroom to the marketplace. He saw the sit-ins as proof that a new generation of student activists was moving to the fore of the civil rights movement and that the black leadership class, epitomized by the NAACP, was no longer the prime agent of black social protest.

Ella Baker, executive director of the SCLC, was so impressed by the enthusiasm and dedication of the emerging student movement that she convinced the SCLC to convene a conference of students conducting sit-ins on Easter weekend (April 15–17, 1960) at Shaw University in Raleigh, North Carolina. Baker hoped to attract 100 students, but 300 showed up, including white students from the North. James Lawson, who had been expelled from Vanderbilt's divinity school for advising the Nashville students to continue their sit-ins, was also present.

The students made it clear that they did not want to be merely adjuncts or junior members of older established groups, like SCLC or the NAACP. Determined to set their own agenda and chart an independent course, the students created (with Baker's encouragement) their own organization, which they called the Student Nonviolent Coordinating Committee (SNCC, pronounced "snick"). Baker immediately recognized the potential of this new army of black and white students from both the North and South determined to rid the country of its scourge of racism and discrimination, not only at lunch counters but in every area of American life.

In Nashville two days after the conclusion of the conference that created SNCC, the bombing of the home of Z. Alexander Looby, the city's first black councilman who was representing students arrested at sit-ins, sent shock waves through the city and galvanized the black community. Although no one was injured, the blast was strong enough to shatter the windows of the building across the street. The bombing solidified the black community and enraged part of the white community as nothing else had. A number of whites, including the mayor of Nashville, denounced the bombing.

To protest the bombing the Nashville Student Movement organized a massive march on city hall—the first major civil rights protest of its kind. About 2,500 people—students and community members—all marched silently. On the steps of city hall in front of television cameras, Diane Nash confronted the mayor. She asked him if he believed it was wrong to discriminate against people solely on the basis of their race or color. The mayor suprised everybody by nodding and saying, yes, he agreed it was wrong.

Nashville merchants were secretly relieved by the mayor's unexpected admission because it helped give them an excuse to try to resolve a growing economic problem, the loss of lunch counter business. The day after the march Martin Luther King, Jr. went to Nashville to praise and support the students. He called the Nashville Student Movement the best organized and most disciplined movement in the country. Three weeks later, on May 10, six Nashville lunch counters began serving blacks.

The role of students and young people in the civil rights movement was crucial to its eventual success, not just in Nashville, but throughout the South. Later Diane Nash said, "The media and history seem to record it as Martin Luther King's movement, but young people should realize that it was people just like them, their age, that formulated goals and strategies, and actually developed the movement."

During the 1960 presidential campaign both candidates—Richard Nixon and John F. Kennedy—tried their best to avoid the civil rights issue since favoring either side would mean losing the backing of an important voting bloc. Support for civil rights would offend southern whites while support for segregation would mean losing the vote of blacks and white liberals. Many blacks were suspicious of Kennedy, who was strongly backed by Governor John Patterson of Alabama and other southern Democratic politicians in favor of segregationist policies.

By October 1960 sit-ins had taken place in 112 southern cities. On October 19 a new round began in Atlanta, where Martin Luther King, Jr. had moved earlier in the year to work more actively as president of the SCLC. One day when King joined a sit-in at a segregated department store restaurant, he was arrested along with the students who were sitting in. The student protesters were released from jail, but not King. Since he was on probation for an earlier arrest for driving without a Georgia license, King was sent to the state penitentiary to serve a four-month sentence.

With the 1960 presidential election less than two weeks away some of Kennedy's political advisers suggested he make a gesture of concern for the jailed civil rights leader. Kennedy placed a courtesy call to King's wife, Coretta, to express his interest, and the candidate's brother Robert Kennedy and his aides called an Atlanta judge and the mayor to see what they could do to get King released. The day after Kennedy called King's wife, he was allowed to leave the penitentiary on bail. The Kennedy campaign printed two million copies of a pamphlet that told the story of Kennedy's call to Mrs. King and had them distributed to black churches and colleges across the country.

The 1960 election turned out to be one of the closest in American history. Kennedy ended up winning the White House by less than one percent of the popular vote. Since more than two-thirds of the black vote went to Kennedy, blacks played an important part in his election. Civil rights leaders and student activists took heart when in his inaugural address in January 1961 the young president told the nation that the torch had been passed to "a new generation of Americans."

However, they were soon disappointed. Not only did the new president propose no new civil rights legislation, but he did not keep his campaign promise to issue an executive order that would end racial discrimination in federally funded housing.

While blacks had played a part in electing the president, so had southern whites. In fact, the "solid Democratic South" was an essential element in the Democratic coalition that had kept Democrats in the White House for all but eight of the previous 28 years. Kennedy's vice-president was Lyndon Johnson of Texas, and southern segregationists, like Governor John Patterson of Alabama, had been among the staunchest supporters of the Kennedy-Johnson ticket. Furthermore, Kennedy needed southern support in Congress, and his hopes for reelection in 1964 depended on his ability to hold on to the support of the Democratic South.

The Kennedy administration faced its first major civil rights challenge in the summer of 1961, when the Congress of Racial Equality (CORE), a Chicago-based civil rights group formed in 1942, undertook a "freedom ride" into the South. The purpose of the ride was to test compliance with the U.S. Supreme Court ruling handed down in late 1960 which supported the integration of bus stations and terminals that served interstate travel. Since the ruling was meaningless without federal enforcement, CORE decided to force the issue by having an interracial group of bus riders travel through the South.

CORE had already undertaken just such a freedom ride in 1947 after the Supreme Court ruled that it was unconstitutional to maintain segregated seating on interstate trains and buses. On that first freedom ride through the upper South, the group of black and white CORE members was harassed and finally arrested for violating state segregation laws.

The strategy for the 1961 freedom ride was to have the blacks sit in the front of the bus and the whites in the back. Then at each stop the whites would enter the waiting room marked "Colored" and the blacks would go into the whites-only waiting room and attempt to use all its facilities. This was not civil disobedience, insisted James Farmer, CORE's executive director, since the Supreme Court had already ruled that segregation at these bus stops was unconstitutional.

Like other civil rights groups, CORE counted on media coverage to educate the public about the bigotry and violence that upheld segregation and to put pressure on the federal government to act. "We planned the Freedom Ride with the specific intention of creating a crisis," he said later. "We were counting on the bigots in the South to do our work for us. We figured that the government would have to respond if we created a situation that was headline news all over the world."

The 13 riders were carefully screened for the trip that began in Washington, D.C. on May 4, 1961. The freedom riders included Farmer, John Lewis, veteran of the Nashville sit-ins and SNCC activist, and James Peck, a 46-year-old white CORE member who had been on the 1947 ride. The plan was to travel for two weeks through the South and arrive in New Orleans on May 17, which was the anniversary of the 1954 Supreme Court school desegregation decision.

Knowing that segregationists would stop at nothing to fight the integration of interstate travel, even though it was the law of the land, some of the freedom riders left letters to be delivered to loved ones if they didn't return. Farmer said they were all prepared for the possibility of death.

In Virginia and the Carolinas scuffles and fights broke out when the freedom riders tried to use the bus stop bathrooms and lunchrooms, but the freedom ride continued. On May 14 in Atlanta, the 13 riders divided into two groups to travel on to Birmingham. At the only scheduled stop along the way in Anniston, Alabama, an angry mob threw rocks at the bus and slashed its tires. The bus raced away, but when it stopped six miles outside Anniston to fix the tires, another mob attacked. Then somebody threw a firebomb into the bus, causing it to burst into flames and forcing the riders to leave through emergency exits. The next day a photograph of the burning bus appeared on the front page of the nation's newspapers.

When the other bus carrying the rest of the group arrived in Birmingham, the city's police were nowhere to be seen. Police commissioner Eugene "Bull" Connor had purposely held back his police to give the angry mob a chance to beat the freedom riders "until it looks like a bulldog got ahold of them." The mob attacked the freedom riders so savagely that one of the riders was paralyzed for life.

The violence against the freedom riders received international as well as national press coverage. The Kennedy administration worried about the bad impression the violence was making abroad, especially in Africa, Asia and Latin America, where the United States was competing with the Soviet Union for the support of Third World countries. Nothing could be worse for American prestige abroad than to have the country's race problems communicated to the rest of the world.

The president called his brother, Attorney General Robert Kennedy, and other members of the Justice Department to a special meeting to see what they could do about the crisis. They discussed the possibility of sending federal marshals to Alabama to maintain order, if necessary. When President Kennedy called Alabama's Governor John Patterson, who had been one of his strongest political supporters, he was told the governor had "gone fishing."

The freedom riders were determined to continue the ride in the face of the mounting violence, but the Greyhound Bus Company refused to drive them out of Birmingham. Fearing for their lives in Birmingham, the freedom riders finally decided to go to the airport and fly to New Orleans. However, that was not the end of the freedom ride because a group of Nashville students—eight blacks and two whites—decided to go to Birmingham to resume the ride. They felt strongly that to give up in the face of intimidation and violence at this stage would set the civil rights movement back and send the wrong message: that if segregationists apply enough violence against blacks, they will back down. The 10 Nashville students arrived in Birmingham prepared to continue the freedom ride.

Robert Kennedy was now determined that the Supreme Court decision upholding the integration of interstate travel be enforced. It was the law of the land, and he was the nation's top law enforcement officer. He communicated this to the bus company and to the Birmingham police. However, no sooner did the new group of student freedom riders arrive in the city when Bull Connor, the Birmingham police commissioner, arrested them, allegedly for their own safety. He sent them to jail, where they protested by going on a hunger strike.

In the middle of their second night in jail the police woke them up and forced them into police cars. They then drove the students to the Tennessee state line and left them there. The students found their way to a phone and called Nashville. The cars that came and picked them up drove them right back to the Birmingham bus station. When they boarded a bus for Montgomery to continue the freedom ride, the driver refused to leave the station.

Governor Patterson, who finally got around to returning the White House phone calls, agreed to meet with John Seigenthaler, a Justice Department official and native Tennessean whom the Kennedy Administration sent to Birmingham to report on the situation. At their meeting the governor, in the presence of his entire cabinet, told Seigenthaler that any attempt by the federal government to send marshals would mean "warfare." However, he said that Alabama was committed to the protection of all visitors who traveled in the state. The head of the state highway patrol assured Seigenthaler that the state police would guard the bus carrying the freedom riders from the time it left Birmingham until it reached the city limits of Montgomery.

On May 20 the new group of freedom riders, now numbering 21, left Birmingham for Montgomery accompanied by state patrol cars and planes overhead. However, as soon as the bus approached Montgomery, the patrol cars and planes disappeared. When the unprotected bus pulled into the Montgomery bus stop, hundreds of angry whites were waiting for the freedom riders. "Kill the niggers!" they shouted.

Jim Zwerg, a white man from Wisconsin, was the first freedom rider to leave the bus. As soon as he got off, the mob grabbed him and beat him senseless. They then attacked the others, including presidential aide John Seigenthaler, who happened to drive into the bus station at that time in his rented car. The mob set several cars on fire before state troopers finally arrived and restored order.

Attorney General Robert Kennedy dispatched 600 federal marshals to an air force base outside Montgomery, a third of whom were immediately sent to the city to protect the freedom riders. Martin Luther King, Jr. flew to Montgomery to address a rally at Ralph Abernathy's church in support of the freedom riders. During the meeting several thousand angry whites surrounded Abernathy's church and threatened the blacks inside.

"We've got an ugly mob outside," King told the packed church. "They have injured some of the federal marshals. They've burned some automobiles. But we are not giving in. Maybe it takes something like this for the federal government to see that Alabama is not going to place any limit on itself—it must be imposed from without." Outside the church federal marshals tried to keep the mob back with tear gas, which drifted into the church and choked many of the blacks trapped inside.

At three in the morning King called Robert Kennedy to inform him of the danger they faced. Kennedy in turn called Governor Patterson and convinced him that the disorder had to be contained. The governor declared martial law and sent state troopers and the Alabama National Guard to disperse the crowd. When it was safe, they escorted people out of the church.

Two days after the siege of the church, a determined group of 27 freedom riders left Montgomery in two buses to continue the freedom ride. When they arrived in Jackson, Mississippi, a very different kind of reception awaited them. Unlike the previous stops, there was no mob waiting for them—only the police, who told them to keep walking right through the white waiting room to the paddy wagons waiting to take them to jail.

The next day the freedom riders were taken to court, where they were quickly tried, convicted and sentenced to 60 days in the state penitentiary. When a new group of freedom riders arrived in Jackson to take their place, they too were arrested. That summer 300 more freedom riders went into the South, where they were arrested and jailed.

✳   ✳   ✳

The Kennedy administration was caught between the two sides. It wanted to support the black struggle for civil rights, but it also wanted to curry favor with the southern wing of the Democratic Party whose political support President Kennedy could ill afford to lose. As news of the jailings of freedom riders spread across the country and the world, Robert Kennedy met with civil rights groups to try to get them to redirect the movement away from violent confrontations that required the administration's intervention. He stressed the need for black voter registration. He believed that black voting power would force southern politicians to pay more attention to the needs of blacks for housing, education and access to public facilities. However, SNCC leaders and other young black activists suspected that the Kennedys wanted to subvert the growing momentum of the civil rights movement.

The freedom rides helped put civil rights in the forefront of national consciousness by offering dramatic proof of the violent lengths to which the forces of segregation would go to resist change, even when the change was mandated by federal law, as it was in the case of interstate travel. Civil rights advocates who had been disappointed by the failure of the Kennedy administration to act could now be more hopeful that the federal government would act to uphold federal law, as it had when it sent federal marshals into the South to protect the freedom riders. Like it or not, the federal government, which had been reluctant to take sides in the controversy, could no longer turn away from the issue.

CHAPTER FOUR NOTES

page 36   "When the Greensboro . . . had come." **Eyes**, p. 129.

page 36   "They must . . . afraid." **Voices**, p. 57.

page 37   "Montgomery . . . did not stumble into it." Quoted in **Civil Rights**, p. 75.

page 38   "The media . . . developed the movement." Quoted in **Civil Rights**, p. 75.

pages 40–41 "We planned . . . all over the world." Quoted in **Bearing**, p. 156.

page 41   "until it looks . . . them." **Civil Rights**, p. 83.

pages 43–44 "We've got . . . from without." **Eyes**, p. 157.

CHAPTER **F**ive

THE MOVEMENT TAKES CENTER STAGE

The Road to Washington

The freedom rides ended the hope of the Kennedy administration that it could remain above the civil rights battle. Its plan to hold together the traditional Democratic coalition forged by Presidents Roosevelt and Truman—labor, blacks and northern liberals and the Democratic Party's traditional power base in the South—suffered a damaging blow when it was forced to send federal marshals to Alabama to protect besieged freedom riders. And that was just the beginning.

By the early 1960s the quest for civil rights was bubbling up in too many places for the nascent movement to be contained by its opponents, moderated by its allies or managed by the civil rights groups themselves. As the spontaneous proliferation of student sit-ins and the rapid growth of SNCC demonstrated, an emerging generation of young black activists was determined to make its voice heard. What began as scattered brushfires at the beginning of the Kennedy years quickly became a roaring blaze that was to capture the attention of the nation and the world.

In 1961 when representatives of the newly formed Student Nonviolent Coordinating Committee (SNCC) went to Albany, Georgia to see if they could mobilize the city's blacks against segregation, that farming center in the southwestern part of the state became the next site of the civil rights struggle.

Blacks made up about half of Albany's 56,000 people, and a fair number of them owned their own businesses—taxi companies, beauty parlors, funeral homes, pool halls and liquor stores—and had children in the local all-black college, Albany State. Many Albany State College students, who already belonged to the NAACP Youth Council, were ripe for civil rights protests after they learned about the sit-ins and freedom rides happening elsewhere.

After the Interstate Commerce Commission issued a ruling banning segregation in interstate bus and train stations, two SNCC workers led a group of Albany State students into the whites-only waiting room of the Trailways bus terminal, where they were arrested, proving that Albany had no intention of abiding by the federal ruling.

In Albany as elsewhere there was disagreement between SNCC and the NAACP over tactics and timing. The local NAACP believed that court action was the key to making lasting progress, while SNCC activists believed that direct action was the best way to challenge segregation. The open defiance of city officials determined to uphold the segregation of the city's bus and train stations against federal law was the opportunity they were waiting for.

The arrest of Albany State students at the city bus terminal prompted a coalition of local black groups called the Albany Movement to hold its first large public meeting in a church. The Albany Movement consisted of such local groups as the Ministerial Alliance, the Negro Voters League and an organization of black professionals called the Criterion Club. The group elected Dr. William Anderson, an osteopath and drug store owner, as its president.

On December 10, 10 freedom riders arrived on a train from Atlanta. When the blacks entered the white waiting room and the whites entered the black waiting room, the city had them all arrested for trespassing. The next day to protest the arrest of the freedom riders, 267 students from Albany State and the local black high school marched to the train station. They were also arrested and put in jail, as were 200 more protesters who marched to city hall two days later. Police chief Laurie Pritchett told reporters he was going to put demonstrators in jails all over Georgia, if he had to. "We can't tolerate the NAACP or the Student Nonviolent Committee or any other nigger organization to take over this town with mass demonstrations."

The arrest of the freedom riders and the students put Albany in the national spotlight. In December after more than 500 protesters had been arrested, the Albany Movement sought outside help. Since Dr. Anderson had gone to school with Martin Luther King, Jr., he called King in Atlanta and invited him to come to Albany and speak at their meeting. King accepted, but he had no intention of staying in Albany overnight. However, at the meeting when Anderson announced a mass march on city hall the following day, King agreed to stay and lead it.

The next day King and Dr. Anderson led 265 demonstrators out of the church toward city hall, but Pritchett and his army of policemen, sheriff's deputies and state troopers blocked their way. Pritchett ordered the marchers to disperse, and when they didn't he arrested them and sent them to jail. King refused bond, vowing to stay in jail until the city desegregated.

Dr. King's arrest received national and international press coverage, further damaging the country's image abroad and opening the way for the Soviet bloc to score more propaganda points. At the height of the Cold War with both East and West vying for the support of the new nations of the Third World, the broadcasting of the country's mistreatment of its black citizens made its call for freedom and democracy around the world sound hollow and hypocritical.

The city commissioners offered to release King and the other jailed protesters, integrate the train and bus terminals and meet with protest leaders if they agreed to stop their demonstrations. After the prisoners were released on bond, King left Albany to give negotiations between local blacks and city officials a chance to work. However, the city officials went back on their word. The talks never took place and the train and bus terminals were never integrated. "We thought that the victory had been won," said King later. "When we got out we discovered it was all a hoax."

When King and Abernathy returned to Albany in February to stand trial for their December arrests, they were found guilty of marching without a permit and ordered to pay either $78 in fines or serve 45 days in jail. Both men chose jail, but three days later they were mysteriously released. Police chief Pritchett claimed an anonymous black man paid their fines, but the truth was that Pritchett secretly arranged to have them released knowing that King's presence in jail would only galvanize local blacks and bring more media attention to the city. Civil rights groups already knew the important role the media played in advancing the civil rights cause, and Pritchett knew it too. King later described his move as "a cunning tactic."

The Kennedy administration followed the events in Albany with great interest. When city officials persisted in their refusal to negotiate with local blacks, President Kennedy said in a nationally televised news conference, "I find it wholly inexplicable why the city council of Albany will not sit down with the citizens of Albany, who may be Negroes, and attempt to secure for them, in a peaceful way, their rights. The U.S. government is involved in sitting down at Geneva with the Soviet Union. I can't understand why the government of Albany . . . cannot do the same for American citizens."

When a federal judge issued a restraining order that specifically ordered King and other leaders of the Albany protest not to march, King was faced with a quandary. King finally decided to obey the federal order on the grounds that even though this particular judge was a segregationist, federal courts were the best friend blacks had. Many of Albany's blacks disagreed, and when 160 marched without King they were arrested and sent to jail.

Four days after the court order to halt the marches was issued, a federal appeals court judge overturned the ruling. The next day 2,000 black demonstrators, many of them young, marched through the streets. Two days later King himself was arrested for leading a prayer meeting in front of city hall. Upon his release two weeks later he left Albany again to let local blacks negotiate with white city officials, but once more the whites refused to meet with local black leaders. When King returned to Albany, the mayor finally agreed to meet with the local leaders. However, once the meeting took place he refused to make any concessions. King was frustrated. Before he left Albany for the final time, all he could do was denounce the intransigence of the city's segregationist officials.

SNCC continued its efforts in Albany and the mass meetings of the Albany Movement continued, but there were no dramatic victories or readily observable results. Albany schools remained segregated, and the city closed the parks rather than let them be integrated. Nonetheless, many Albany blacks felt they had won a moral victory. Dr. Anderson regarded the Albany campaign as "an overwhelming success" that changed forever the attitude of the local people, especially young people.

Although the SCLC learned many valuable lessons from the Albany campaign and the group's presence in the city attracted national and international attention, it left having failed to make much of a lasting difference. Afterward Dr. King felt discouraged that all his efforts failed to produce the dramatic victory he worked so hard to achieve. He felt betrayed by the segregationist judge who had ruled against them and blamed the Kennedy administration for having appointed him to the federal bench.

While in Albany King learned for the first time how hostile the director of the FBI, J. Edgar Hoover, was toward the SCLC and toward King personally. Hoover was convinced that King was under the influence of Communists and tried to convince the White House that King and his associates were stirring up trouble to make America look bad in the eyes of the rest of the world. Andrew Young of the SCLC said that King left Albany "very depressed." He and the SCLC knew they needed a clear-cut victory to lift their spirits and energize them for the battles ahead.

In Mississippi—as elsewhere in the South—the first stirrings of civil rights activity took place without the glare of media coverage. Mississippi was poor and backward with fewer doctors, nurses and lawyers per capita than any other state in the nation. Life was especially difficult for blacks, who made up almost half the population. In rural counties black families lived close to starvation in unpainted frame shanties and tar-paper shacks and were kept "in their place" by intimidation and violence.

Mississippi led the nation in beatings, lynchings and disappearances. What made the 1955 murder of Emmett Till, who was visiting from Chicago, unusual was the fact that it received national attention—unlike the thousands of previous murders of

Mississippi blacks who were lynched, shot, beaten to death or simply disappeared without a trace. Blacks had long been kept from voting by threats, intimidation and murder. Only five percent of Mississippi blacks were registered to vote—the lowest rate in the nation.

In the summer of 1961 a group of SNCC student volunteers under the leadership of Robert Moses, a 26-year-old teacher from New York City, went to McComb in Pike County at the invitation of the head of the local NAACP. They set out to help the NAACP organize a month-long voter registration drive with classes to teach blacks how to register. When more SNCC activists arrived, a similar registration drive was organized in nearby Amite County.

Resistance by local whites was immediate. Moses was arrested when he accompanied three people to the registration office. Later when local black youngsters who had attended a workshop for teenagers staged a sit-in at the local Woolworth's whites-only lunch counter, they were arrested, expelled from school and sent to jail, some for as long as eight months. Fifteen-year-old Brenda Travis was sentenced to a year in a state institution for delinquents.

On September 25 after a white man killed Herbert Lee, who served as Moses' driver in Amite County, Moses and other SNCC workers led more than 100 black high school students in a protest against the murder of their friend and the release of the accused man. They were arrested and the students were expelled from school. Later when Moses and his SNCC colleagues held classes for the expelled students, they were arrested for contributing to the delinquency of minors and sentenced to four months in jail.

When the local NAACP became disturbed that the SNCC demonstrations were shifting the focus away from voter registration, they asked SNCC to leave. After their release from jail in December, the last of the SNCC activists left McComb. By then SNCC had already set its sights on its new campaign in Albany, Georgia.

In the fall of 1962, white Mississippi faced a much greater challenge when on September 3 a federal district court ordered the University of Mississippi to admit James Meredith as a student. Meredith, a native Mississippian and a college sophomore at all-black Jackson State, had wanted to attend the university since the age of 12 when he was in the office of a white doctor he respected and saw a college picture of him in his Ole Miss football uniform.

When he sought the help of the NAACP in Mississippi, the organization put him in contact with Thurgood Marshall, head of the NAACP Legal Defense Fund. By the time Marshall and the NAACP filed his request in federal court, Meredith had nine years of military service behind him as a staff sergeant in the U.S. Air Force and 12 college courses to his credit.

Reacting the way Orval Faubus had five years earlier during the school desegregation crisis in Little Rock, Governor Ross Barnett went on statewide television to attack the federal court and rally opposition against its ruling. Calling it "our greatest crisis since the War Between the States," Barnett blamed "an ambitious federal government employing naked and arbitrary power." The governor said defiantly, "I hereby direct each official to uphold segregation laws enacted by the state of Mississippi, regardless of the federal courts."

When James Meredith went to the campus to register for his classes on September 20, the governor was there to block the door. After the university registrar read a proclamation by the trustees that designated Governor Barnett acting registrar, the governor told Meredith his application for admission was not accepted. When Meredith, flanked by the chief federal marshal and a lawyer from the Justice Department, returned five days later to try to register once more, he was refused again.

After behind-the-scenes calls between the Kennedy administration and Governor Barnett failed to defuse the confrontation, President Kennedy dispatched U.S. Army troops to Memphis and called up the Mississippi National Guard into federal service. On Sunday evening, September 30, the U.S. government moved to enforce the federal court order. Federal marshals and other government officials took up positions on the Oxford campus, and federal troops in Tennessee and the Mississippi National Guard were put on alert. A government plane flew Meredith from Memphis to Oxford, where Deputy Attorney General Nicholas Katzenbach met him at the airport and escorted him in a convoy of military trucks to the campus. He was taken secretly to Baxter Hall where 24 federal marshals guarded the room, where he waited alone through the night.

When the thousands of white students and townspeople who had converged on Oxford from all over the state learned Meredith was on campus, they went on a rampage, throwing rocks and bottles, breaking windows and overturning cars. The state troopers who had been on duty fled the violence, leaving the vastly outnumbered federal marshals to face the mob.

President Kennedy went on national television to urge Mississippians and the Ole Miss students to remain calm. But the mob became more violent as the rioters threw bricks, acid and flaming missiles and shot at the marshals who tried to hold them off with tear gas. A correspondent for a French news agency was shot in the back of the head at close range, and a spectator from a nearby town was also killed.

At about ten o'clock, Deputy Attorney General Katzenbach urgently requested the White House to send federal troops to Oxford immediately. The president gave the order, but by the time the troops reached the campus and took up positions at four o'clock in the morning, most of the damage was already done. Half of the 320 federal marshals were injured, 28 of them by gunshots.

Early in the morning with the littered grounds of Ole Miss looking like a Civil War battlefield, federal marshals escorted Meredith across the campus to register. Meeting no resistance, he went to his first class in American history at nine o'clock.

Federal marshals remained on campus to protect Meredith for the rest of the year. He endured harassment, insults and isolation, but there were also occasional demonstrations of support. A few white students defied campus sentiment by saying hello to him when he crossed the campus or by sitting down at his table in the dining hall. In the summer of 1963—nine years after the Supreme Court declared segregation in schools unconstitutional—the University of Mississippi awarded James Meredith his bachelor's degree in political science.

After Meredith enrolled at Ole Miss, Mississippi civil rights workers began hoping the federal government would openly support them in their battle against segregation. The head of the NAACP Youth Council in Jackson said that for the first time in

Protected by federal marshals, James Meredith attends his first day of class at the previously all-white University of Mississippi in Oxford on October 1, 1962. *(Library of Congress)*

their lives blacks in the state witnessed a victory for one of their own. The Meredith success heightened interest in the civil rights struggle, especially among young people.

*   *   *

After their disappointing campaign in Albany, SCLC's Fred Shuttlesworth convinced Martin Luther King, Jr. that their next target should be Birmingham, Alabama's largest city and a major steel and business center. Blacks made up 40 percent of the city's population of 350,000, but because they were denied good jobs their average income was less than half that of whites.

Birmingham's reputation as the most segregated city in America had been confirmed by the violent mob attack on freedom riders in 1961 that forced President Kennedy to send federal marshals to the city. One year later when a federal court ordered the desegregation of Birmingham's public facilities, the city closed its parks, playgrounds, swimming pools and public golf courses rather than comply.

Shuttlesworth, a veteran civil rights activist and leader of a group called the Alabama Christian Movement for Human

Rights, knew Birmingham all too well. When he tried to enroll his children in a white school, a mob beat him and stabbed his wife while white policemen looked on. In 1956 when a bomb destroyed his home, nobody was arrested. Between 1957 and 1963 there were 18 unsolved bombings in the city's black neighborhoods, earning the city the nickname of "Bombingham." Shuttlesworth convinced the SCLC that Birmingham was ripe for a major civil rights campaign.

At a three-day SCLC retreat in Georgia, Shuttlesworth, King, Abernathy and other SCLC members worked out a careful plan for what they called Project C (for "Confrontation")—with Birmingham's downtown business district as its primary target—to begin in March 1963.

Martin Luther King, Jr. traveled the country to raise bail money for the campaign, while Shuttlesworth and Wyatt Walker worked on the details of Project C. They studied city laws and regulations about demonstrations and the routes to the targeted

Reverend Martin Luther King, Jr. and Reverend Ralph Abernathy led the 1963 Southern Christian Leadership Conference (SCLC) desegregation campaign in Birmingham, Alabama, which many considered the most segregated city in America. *(Library of Congress)*

downtown stores from the Sixteenth Street Baptist Church, which was going to be the campaign's headquarters. Walker surveyed the targeted lunchrooms and restaurants in order to count the stools, counters, tables and chairs and decide on the best ways for the demonstrators to enter and leave.

The Project C demonstrations began on April 3, 1963 and intensified over Palm Sunday weekend. The protesters marched, sang freedom songs, picketed and prayed in the streets. On Saturday, April 6, Shuttlesworth and a group of 30 demonstrators who marched on city hall were arrested and sent to jail. On Palm Sunday, the next day, police used dogs and nightsticks to break up a prayer march through the downtown streets led by Martin Luther King, Jr.'s younger brother, A.D. King.

In response to police commissioner Eugene "Bull" Connor, who went to court to seek an injunction against further demonstrations, an Alabama circuit court judge ordered 133 civil rights leaders, including King, Abernathy and Shuttlesworth, not to take part in or encourage any further marches, sit-ins, picketing or other kinds of demonstrations. However, Dr. King decided to defy the order. On Good Friday, when he led a march of 50 demonstrators downtown, television cameras captured the dramatic scene of King being arrested, put in a police van and driven off to jail where he was placed in solitary confinement.

The *Birmingham News* printed a full-page open letter by eight local white clergymen that criticized King for the Birmingham campaign. Writing from his cell in the margins of the newspaper and on pieces of toilet paper, Dr. King answered their letter with a letter of his own.

His letter, addressed to "My Dear Fellow Clergymen," began: "While confined here in the Birmingham city jail, I came across your recent statement calling my present activities 'unwise and untimely'. . . . since I feel that you are men of genuine good will and that your criticisms are sincerely set forth, I want to try to answer your statement in what I hope will be patient and reasonable terms.

"We know through painful experience that freedom is never voluntarily given by the oppressor; it must be demanded by the oppressed. Frankly, I have yet to engage in a direct-action campaign that was well-timed in the view of those who have not suffered unduly from the disease of segregation. For years now I have heard the word `Wait!' It rings in the ears of every Negro with piercing familiarity. This `Wait' has almost always meant `Never.'"

King went on in the letter—later published as "Letter from a Birmingham Jail"—to explain why the fight against segregation should not be delayed. "Perhaps it is easy for those who have never felt the stinging darts of segregation to say, `Wait.' But when you have seen vicious mobs lynch your mothers and fathers at will and drown your sisters and brothers at whim; when you have seen hate-filled policemen curse, kick, and even kill your black brothers and sisters; when you see the vast majority of your twenty million Negro brothers smothering in an airtight cage of poverty in the midst of an affluent society; when you suddenly find your tongue twisted and your speech stammering as you seek to explain to your six-year-old daughter why she can't go to the public amusement park that has just been advertised on television . . . then you will find it difficult to wait. I hope, sirs," concluded King, "you can understand our legitimate and unavoidable impatience. . . ."

After King and Abernathy were released on bond after eight days in jail, they joined their SCLC colleagues in preparing for the next phase of the campaign. James Bevel, a veteran of the Nashville sit-ins, urged that children be allowed to demonstrate. He argued that children could not be fired from jobs the way their parents could, and the sight of black children getting arrested and sent to jail was sure to stir the country's conscience. After the meeting SCLC workers fanned out over the city to recruit black schoolchildren for the next wave of marches.

On May 2 a new chapter in the civil rights movement began when an army of children—ranging in age from 6 to 18—left the church in groups and set off for downtown singing freedom songs. The police arrested them and put them in paddy wagons. When the groups of children kept coming out of the church, Connor had to use school buses to hold them all. By the end of the day Birmingham jails were filled with 959 black children.

The next day when more than 1,000 children assembled at the church, Bull Connor's police and city firefighters were waiting. When the children came out of the church and started to march,

Connor ordered the firefighters to turn their hoses on them. Water powerful enough to rip the bark off trees knocked down the marchers and slammed them against buildings and cars.

Media coverage of Bull Connor's brutal attack, using fire hoses and police dogs on children, shocked the nation and the world. Local blacks who had questioned the wisdom of the demonstrations now strongly supported them. Priests, ministers and rabbis from around the country went to Birmingham to show their support. By May 6 more than 2,000 demonstrators were in jail.

The Kennedy administration, which had no authority to intervene, once again had to worry about the terrible impression this violence against American citizens was making on the rest of the world. The president dispatched his aide Burke Marshall to Birmingham to encourage negotiations between the demonstrators and the city's white business community. The business leaders who disapproved of the confrontational tactics of Bull Connor and his police and worried about further loss of business and damage to their stores met with the SCLC to resolve the crisis.

They agreed to desegregate the lunch counters and hire black workers, but when the agreement was made public on Monday, May 10, it caused a firestorm. Bull Connor and the other city commissioners denounced it and called for a white boycott of any downtown store that agreed to desegregate. At a night rally outside the city, 1,000 Ku Klux Klansmen in white robes denounced the agreement, burned crosses and made racist speeches.

Late at night somebody in a car threw a bomb at the home of A.D. King, and a few hours later the motel where Martin Luther King and his SCLC associates were staying was also bombed. Four people were injured, but Dr. King escaped unharmed. Angry blacks quickly filled the streets around the motel and pelted the police with bricks and rocks. Wyatt Walker tried to get the people to go home, but the rioting continued and several stores were set on fire.

To help restore order President Kennedy sent federal troops to Fort McClellan, 30 miles from Birmingham, saying he refused to allow the agreement worked out between the city's business leaders and the SCLC to be sabotaged by a few extremists. The president promised that the federal government would do all it could to preserve order, protect lives and uphold the law. In what proved to be the largest, best organized, most effective campaign yet, the federal government once again weighed in on the side of the civil rights movement against those who would continue to deny American citizens their most basic rights.

*   *   *

In the meantime, Mississippi's NAACP field secretary, Medgar Evers, told the mayor of Jackson and the city's Chamber of Commerce that the NAACP was going to use "all legal means of protest" to desegregate stores, businesses and public facilities in the state capital. With the SCLC challenging segregation in Birmingham, Evers thought it was time for bolder action in Mississippi.

Born and raised in the state, Evers had served in the armed forces in World War II. After he attended Alcorn Agricultural and Mechanical College, he applied to the all-white University of Mississippi law school. Even though the Supreme Court had just ruled that segregated schools were unconstitutional, the law school rejected Evers on the grounds that his letters of recommendation were not from white people.

Evers then went to work for the NAACP. As its first Mississippi field secretary, he traveled the state to investigate the disappearances and murders of rural blacks that the local police brushed aside as "accidents." As a result, he and his family lived under constant threat of violence. They kept the blinds drawn at home, and he taught his wife and children what to do if they heard shooting or if people forced their way into the house.

One of the biggest obstacles Evers faced in his work was overcoming the fear that so many blacks in the state felt after years of beatings, burnings and lynchings. Many blacks told him they couldn't join the NAACP because if they did they would be fired from their jobs. Even the black newspaper in Jackson advised its readers to keep their distance from Evers and the NAACP.

After the state university was forced to admit Meredith, Evers organized a boycott of the Mississippi State Fair in Jackson. The purpose of the boycott was to protest the fact that the first week of the fair was exclusively for whites, and blacks were only allowed in for the last three days of the event. Evers was suprised and encouraged by the fact that more blacks boycotted the fair than attended.

Medgar Evers of the NAACP, a civil rights leader in
Mississippi, was murdered in the driveway of his home
on June 13, 1963. *(Library of Congress)*

When the SCLC successfully challenged segregation in Birmingham, he decided the time was ripe for a similar campaign in Jackson. On May 28, the NAACP-sponsored sit-in at the lunch counter at Woolworth's downtown store and the attack against the demonstrators by an angry mob of whites drew national press coverage. When the mayor of Jackson indicated a willingness to talk with a group of black clergymen, the White Citizens' Council and Mississippi state legislators pressured him to change his mind. Medgar Evers' home was bombed, and when student demonstrators resumed the sit-in at the Woolworth lunch counter, the police beat them and sent them to jail.

The brutal attacks on civil rights demonstrators in Birmingham and Jackson that spring made a strong impression on white America and did much to win them over to the civil rights cause. Day after day, week after week, black American citizens demonstrated peacefully for their constitutional rights only to be beaten, shot, arrested and put in jail.

*   *   *

In Alabama, Governor Wallace, Birmingham police commissioner Bull Connor and the other defenders of segregation faced a new problem when a federal court ordered the University of Alabama to admit two black students. On June 11, 1963, when the students arrived at the university to register, Governor Wallace blocked the door. Like Governors Faubus of Arkansas and Barnett of Mississippi before him, Wallace sought to make himself popular with the white voters of his state by standing up to the federal government.

In front of the television cameras he told Deputy Attorney General Nicholas Katzenbach and the federal marshals who accompanied the students that the issue of enrollment in the University of Alabama was the business of the state, not the federal government. However, after he scored his political points, he declined to challenge the authority of the federal government, backed up by U.S. marshals and the Alabama National Guard. The two black students were allowed to enroll.

The next night—June 12—President Kennedy went on television to address the nation:

On June 11, 1963, Governor George Wallace (left) blocked the door at the University of Alabama to prevent two black students from registering despite a federal court order that they be admitted. The governor told Deputy Attorney General Nicholas Katzenbach (right) that the issue of enrollment in the university was state, not federal, business. *(Library of Congress)*

We are confronted primarily with a moral issue. It is as old as the Scriptures and as clear as the American Constitution. The heart of the question is whether all Americans are afforded equal rights and equal opportunities; whether we are going to treat our fellow Americans as we want to be treated. If an American because his skin is dark cannot eat lunch in a restaurant open to the public, if he cannot send his children to the best public school available, if he cannot vote for the public officials who represent him, if in short he cannot enjoy the full and free life which all of us want, then who among us would be content to have the color of his skin changed and stand in his place? Who among us would then be content with the counsels of patience and delay?

The president announced that he was submitting to Congress legislation that would give to all Americans "the right to be served in facilities which are open to the public—hotels, restaurants, theaters, retail stores, and similar establishments." He called it a basic right whose denial was "an arbitrary indignity that no American in 1963 should have to endure."

*　　*　　*

That same night in Jackson, Myrlie Evers listened to the president's speech with her children as she waited for her husband to return home. Later when Evers arrived, she said, "We heard him get out of the car and the car door slam, and in that same instant, we heard the loud gunfire. The children fell to the floor, as he had taught them to, and I made a run for the front door, turned on the light, and there he was." Myrlie saw his body on the ground and screamed. Neighbors helped her drive him to the hospital, but it was too late. Evers was dead.

The funeral service in Jackson attracted thousands of mourners. Evers, a World War II veteran, was buried in Arlington National Cemetery. The day after the burial President Kennedy received Myrlie and her children in the White House. He expressed his condolences and gave small gifts to the children, telling them they should be proud of their father.

The accused killer, Byron De La Beckwith, was tried twice and both trials ended in hung juries despite overwhelming evidence that he committed the murder and his own boastings about it. While being held during the trial, De La Beckwith was given all the comforts of home, including a television set and typewriter and the right to come and go as he pleased. During the first trial, Governor Barnett visited the courtroom to shake hands with the accused killer. When De La Beckwith went home, the town welcomed him with banners and had a parade in his honor. He was so popular in the state that he later ran for lieutenant governor. More than 30 years later, De La Beckwith was tried again. On February 5, 1994, a jury of eight blacks and four whites—after six hours of deliberation—reached a guilty verdict. For the murder of Medgar Evers, De La Beckwith, 73, was sentenced to life in prison.

One week after he addressed the nation, President Kennedy submitted to Congress a civil rights bill that called for equal access to public accommodations and gave the attorney general the authority to initiate school desegregation suits and shut off funds to any federal programs that practiced discrimination.

✻   ✻   ✻

The next day Martin Luther King, Jr., speaking in Alabama, indicated for the first time in public his interest in black labor leader A. Philip Randolph's idea of a massive demonstration in Washington. He thought a march on the nation's capital on behalf of jobs and freedom by civil rights supporters and their labor allies might help pressure Congress to pass the civil rights bill.

Randolph, the 74-year-old head of the Brotherhood of Sleeping Car Porters, who had spent his life working to secure rights and economic opportunity for black people, had first proposed such a march on the nation's capital in 1941 when it looked as if the United States might enter the world war and there would be even more jobs in the booming defense industries. Randolph wanted to make sure blacks got their fair share of the new jobs, especially since defense industries openly discriminated against blacks. He figured a large demonstration in the nation's capital would put political pressure on the Roosevelt administration to open up defense industry jobs to blacks.

Randolph hired Bayard Rustin, a young black man who attended the College of the City of New York, to publicize the march and organize march committees in different parts of the country. The pressure worked because on June 20, 1941—two weeks before the scheduled march—President Roosevelt signed an executive order that banned discrimination in the war industries and established the Fair Employment Practices Commission as a forum for blacks who had been discriminated against to air their complaints. Having achieved his goal, Randolph called off the march.

After the war Randolph launched a campaign to integrate the military by forming the Committee Against Segregation in the Armed Forces. In 1948, after Randolph met personally with President Truman to discuss the matter, the president signed an executive order that integrated the U.S. military.

In the early 1960s Randolph worried that the growing civil rights movement was not focusing enough on the economic goals Randolph believed in. Black unemployment was double that of whites, while the average income of a black family was half of what it was for a white family. Randolph believed that what blacks around the country needed most were jobs and more economic power.

In the fall of 1962 Randolph resurrected his idea of a mass march on Washington. He suggested to Rustin that they organize a march to be called the Emancipation March for Jobs, which would take place on January 1, 1963—the 100th anniversary of the Emancipation Proclamation, which President Lincoln issued during the Civil War, freeing the slaves. However, when the idea didn't interest the leaders of the civil rights movement, Randolph and Rustin changed the name of their proposed march to the March on Washington for Jobs and Freedom. The day after King's public statement Randolph moved quickly. On his instructions, Cleveland Robinson, a New York City labor leader, held a press conference at which he announced that the march would take place.

When President Kennedy heard about the plan, he invited civil rights and labor leaders to the White House to talk them out of the idea. The historic meeting in the Cabinet Room on June 22, 1963 was a measure of how much progress the civil rights movement had made in such a short time. Attending the meeting were the president, Vice President Johnson, Attorney General Robert Kennedy, and the nation's foremost civil rights leaders—Randolph, King, Roy Wilkins of the NAACP, Whitney Young of the Urban League and James Farmer of CORE. Walter Reuther, the white president of the United Auto Workers, was also there, representing labor.

The president explained that his civil rights bill faced an uphill battle in Congress since Southern senators could keep the bill from ever coming to a vote by using the filibuster, and that a march on Washington could do more harm than good. "We want success in Congress," he said, "not just a big show at the Capitol."

Randolph pointed out that a large peaceful demonstration in Washington would channel black hopes for a better life and show the country the strength of their numbers and the justice of their cause. King and Farmer also spoke in favor of the march, convincing the others it was a good idea. The White House meeting that the Kennedy administration hoped would stop the march ended up convincing the civil rights leaders that it should go forward.

Leaders of the March on Washington of August 28, 1963
included Martin Luther King, Jr., Roy Wilkins of the NAACP,
A. Philip Randolph of the Brotherhood of Sleeping Car
Porters and Walter Reuther of the UAW. *(Library of Congress)*

When Randolph recommended that Bayard Rustin organize
the march, Wilkins warned him that criticism of the controversial
Rustin could hurt the march. Rustin had once been a member of
the Young Communist League, and was a pacifist who had been
a conscientious objector during World War II. Rustin was also an
open homosexual. Randolph defended Rustin and convinced the
others he was the best person for the job.

In return for their support on the issue of Rustin, Randolph
agreed to the request of the others that whites be included in the
leadership of the march. The civil rights movement depended on
the support of progressive whites, and Wilkins and Young were
especially insistent on having white participation as a way to
broaden support for the march. As a result, the so-called Big
Six—Randolph, King, Wilkins, Young, Farmer, and John Lewis of
SNCC—added four white members: Mathew Ahmann, executive
director of the National Catholic Conference for Interracial Justice;
Dr. Eugene Carson Blake, vice chairman of the Commission on Race
Relations of the National Council of Churches; Rabbi Joachim

Prinz, president of the American Jewish Congress; and Walter Reuther of the UAW, representing the labor movement.

The expanded group—the Top Ten—chose August 28 as the date for the march, which they agreed would begin on the Mall near the Washington Monument and proceed for one mile to the Lincoln Memorial for the main program. They all agreed the march was to be a peaceful show of black and white Americans marching together for justice and equal rights.

Bayard Rustin had been working for human rights all his life and had been arrested 22 times. He helped found CORE and SCLC and was on CORE's first freedom ride in 1947. He had traveled to India to study the nonviolent philosophy of Mohandas Gandhi and knew personally many of the leaders of the emerging nations of Africa. He was a superb organizer, having organized many human rights events around the world, including a peace walk in England, an anti-nuclear march in France and a demonstration against anti-Semitism in West Germany.

Two days after he was named deputy director of the march, Rustin set up his headquarters in Harlem and formed an operating committee to handle all aspects of the march—publicity, fundraising, transportation and working with authorities in Washington. With less than two months to organize the march Rustin attended to the thousands of details connected with handling the needs of the 100,000 people they hoped would join the march—security, food, phones, toilets, parking, medical emergencies and instructions and information for the marchers. He anticipated every contingency and left nothing to chance. "If you want to organize anything," he said, "assume that everybody is absolutely stupid. And assume yourself that you're stupid."

Many people left for Washington well ahead of time. A group from the Brooklyn chapter of CORE made the 237-mile trip on foot, setting out two weeks ahead of time with signs that read "We March from New York City for Freedom." An 82-year-old man from Dayton, Ohio rode his bicycle, and another man from Chicago roller-skated wearing a flaming red sash that said "Freedom." Cars set out from as far away as California, and special trains and buses left St. Louis, Chicago, Detroit, Birmingham, Jacksonville and other cities.

On the day of the march itself, August 28, 1963, at 1:30 in the morning the first of a series of 450 chartered buses left the armory on 143rd Street in Harlem, New York City. An hour later 80 buses provided by CORE left 125th Street. A little later a special 14-car train left New York's Penn Station. More than 40 special trains, 2,200 chartered buses and many thousands of cars transported people to Washington.

Although the large AFL-CIO labor organization declined to support the march officially, individual unions within the AFL-CIO participated, such as Reuther's UAW, the International Ladies Garment Workers Union (ILGWU), the Union of Electrical Workers, the Communication Workers of America and Randolph's Brotherhood of Sleeping Car Porters.

Well-known entertainers performed for the crowd as it gathered at the Washington Monument in preparation for the mile-long march to the Lincoln Memorial, where the civil rights leaders were to deliver their speeches. The celebrities included actors Sidney Poitier, Charlton Heston, Marlon Brando, Paul Newman, Ruby Dee, Burt Lancaster, Diahann Carroll, singers Marian Anderson, Harry Belafonte, Lena Horne, Joan Baez, Bob Dylan, Peter, Paul, and Mary, comedian Dick Gregory, writer James Baldwin, baseball great Jackie Robinson and his son, and Dr. Ralph Bunche, United Nations diplomat and the first black American to win the Nobel Prize for Peace.

The crowd of 200,000 people that began the march at the Washington Monument swelled to about 250,000 by the time it reached the Lincoln Memorial. For the speeches special seats were reserved for members of Congress. The idea of the march became politically acceptable so quickly that only 92 of the more than 535 members of Congress—mostly southern—ended up staying away.

No event in American history was more extensively covered by the media—not even a presidential inauguration. The 40 television cameras set up at the Lincoln Memorial to cover the speeches made it the largest outdoor TV operation ever undertaken. The Voice of America broadcast the event around the world. Thousands of newspaper reporters and photographers for the national and international press were also on hand. When the marchers reached the Lincoln Memorial and the program began, all the major television networks interrupted their programming to provide continuous live coverage.

The nation's capital had never seen anything like it: a quarter million people of all kinds—blacks, whites, Jews, gentiles, men, women, children, babies, grandparents, ministers, priests, nuns, rabbis—demonstrating for equality. The intense media coverage communicated to the country and the world the impressive strengths of the young civil rights movement—its idealism, seriousness of purpose and commitment to nonviolence. Many of the marchers wore suits and dresses to underscore the dignity of the occasion. A white woman from South Carolina watching from the sidelines told a reporter, "I'm not sympathetic to all the purposes of this demonstration, but I must say they can teach this nation a lesson in good manners."

When A. Philip Randolph stepped up to the podium, the crowd greeted him warmly in recognition of his role as the author of the march and "grand old man" of the black struggle. He urged his listeners to carry the civil rights movement back home with them into every nook and cranny of the country. The roar that went up at the end of his speech was the crowd's tribute to the man whose longtime dream had at last come true. A tribute to women in the civil rights movement—Rosa Parks, Diane Nash Bevel, Daisy Bates and Myrlie Evers—and speeches by others followed.

The climax of the march was Dr. King's now famous "I Have a Dream" speech. The crowd responded to his speech with such emotion that he departed from his prepared text and told them about his dream, "deeply rooted in the American dream, that one day this nation will rise up and live out the true meaning of its creed—we hold these truths to be self-evident, that all men are created equal."

Making up this part of his speech as he went along, he elaborated on his vision of the future.

> When we allow freedom to ring, when we let it ring
> from every village and every hamlet, from every state
> and every city, we will be able to speed up that day
> when all of God's children—black men and white men,
> Jews and Gentiles, Protestants and Catholics—will be
> able to join hands and sing in the words of the old

At the March on Washington on August 28, 1963, an estimated 250,000 people moved from the Washington Monument (in the distance) to the Lincoln Memorial (the steps can be seen in the foreground), where Martin Luther King, Jr. gave his "I Have a Dream" speech. *(Library of Congress)*

Negro spiritual, *"Free at last, free at last, thank God Almighty, we are free at last."*

King's speech made a profound impression on the crowd and on the 80 million Americans who watched it live on television, most of whom never heard King speak before. At the end of the speech there was a stunned silence. Then people cheered, and many wept openly.

The March on Washington marked the coming of age of the civil rights movement by successfully putting the long deferred issue of racial justice at the top of the nation's political agenda. However, many major battles lay ahead, not only in the halls of Congress, but in cities, towns and villages across America. Just how dangerous the enemies of racial justice were and the ugly lengths to which they would go were demonstrated in Alabama three weeks after the march. On September 15 at the Sixteenth Street Baptist Church in Birmingham—where the civil rights demonstrators had set off on their marches the previous spring—a bomb blast killed four young girls who were attending Sunday school. Dr. King's dream was a long way from fulfillment.

CHAPTER FIVE NOTES

page 49   "We can't tolerate . . . mass demonstrations. " **Parting**, p. 537.

page 49   "We thought . . . hoax." **Eyes**, p. 170.

page 50   "a cunning tactic." **Eyes**, p. 172.

page 50   "I find it . . . American citizens." Quoted in **Bearing**, p. 212.

page 53   "our greatest crisis . . . an ambitious federal . . . I hereby direct . . . federal courts." **Road**, p. 61.

pages 57–58 "While confined . . . meant `Never' . . . Perhaps it is . . . unavoidable impatience . . ." Quoted in **Eyes**, pp. 187–189.

page 60   "all legal means of protest." **Voices**, p. 154.

page 63   "We are confronted . . . delay?" Quoted in *James Haskins*, **The March on Washington**. New York: HarperCollins, 1993, p. 26.

pages 63–64 "the right . . . an arbitrary . . . have to endure." **Eyes**, p. 195.

page 64   "We heard him . . . there he was." **Voices**, p. 154.

page 66   "We want success . . . at the Capitol." **Bearing**, p. 271.

page 68   "If you want . . . you're stupid." **March**, p. 64.

page 70   "I'm not sympathetic . . . good manners." **March**, p. 89.

pages 70–72 "deeply rooted . . . I have a dream . . . free at last.'" Quoted in **March**, p. 107.

CHAPTER Six

VOTING RIGHTS

Mississippi, Selma and the Voting Rights Act of 1965

Since the end of Reconstruction the South kept blacks from voting by means of poll taxes, literacy tests, grandfather clauses and intimidation and violence. Few blacks dared to register when they knew it would lead to some form of retribution, and perhaps even cost them their lives.

Nowhere in the country were blacks more disenfranchised than in Mississippi, where more than 95 percent were unregistered voters, and the white people in charge of the state did everything in their power to keep it that way. SNCC activist Allard Lowenstein said that the reason the whites who ran Mississippi didn't allow free elections was that if they did they would no longer be running the state.

The Mississippi state constitution stated that to vote a person had to "read *or* interpret" the state constitution, but in 1954 the state legislature changed the requirement from "read or interpret" to "read *and* interpret." That put even more power in the hands of the white registrars to turn away prospective black voters.

Often the blacks who tried to register were more educated than the registrars who challenged them. One black teacher who went to register listened as the registration official struggled to read the test questions. When she finally broke in and told him the words he was having trouble with were "constitutionality" and "interrogatory," he got angry and told her she failed the test.

For years the NAACP in Mississippi had been trying to help blacks register, but without much success. The SNCC workers who went to McComb and Amite counties in 1961 to help blacks register had to leave with little to show for their efforts.

However, the following year—1962—things began to change when SNCC received funding from the Voter Education Project for a statewide voter registration drive. Local civil rights activists joined forces with SNCC, NAACP, SCLC and CORE representatives to create the Council of Federated Organizations (COFO). In the fall of 1963, COFO launched a project called Freedom Vote whose purpose was to give blacks practice in registering and voting and thereby to demonstrate to white Mississippi and the federal government that blacks wanted to vote, segregationist claims to the contrary notwithstanding.

Since blacks were not registered to vote for governor in the state's November election, the Freedom Vote project created a make-believe election to give blacks experience voting. In this practice election blacks could vote either for the official Democratic or Republican candidates that whites would be voting for or for the candidates of the unofficial "Freedom Party." The Freedom Party candidates for governor and lieutenant governor were Aaron Henry, a black pharmacist who was president of the Mississippi NAACP, and the Reverend Edwin King, the white chaplain at the all-black Tougaloo College. The idea behind the mock election was to raise the political consciousness of blacks and get them interested in voting by having them take part in the election as if their vote counted.

SNCC activists Bob Moses and Allard Lowenstein recruited 60 white students from Stanford and Yale universities to come to Mississippi to get out the vote for the project on the assumption that "national sentiments would not tolerate assaults against white students, especially those from leading colleges and prominent families." The students spent two weeks in Mississippi going door-to-door informing blacks about the "election" and encouraging them to cast their ballots at tables the Freedom Vote project set up on street corners and in barbershops and beauty parlors around the state. Despite harassment, arrests and beatings, 93,000 blacks voted statewide in the Freedom Vote election. They voted overwhelmingly for Henry and King.

COFO planned an even more ambitious voting rights project for the following summer. The project, known as Freedom Summer, called for a massive voter registration drive across Mississippi. Some SNCC staff members had reservations about inviting hundreds of student volunteers, but most Mississippi blacks liked the idea of having the idealistic, energetic students come to the state.

Unlike the Freedom Vote project, Freedom Summer was designed to register blacks for a real election—the 1964 presidential election. The ambitious goals of the project were to register as many blacks as possible across the state; organize a "Freedom Democratic Party" to challenge the official whites-only Mississippi Democratic Party; set up "freedom schools" for black children, most of whom didn't attend school because they had to work in the fields; and establish community centers for blacks who needed medical or legal help. Student volunteers were recruited at Ivy League colleges in the Northeast, large universities in the Midwest and black colleges in the South.

As Freedom Summer approached, white Mississippi braced itself for what Jackson newspapers called an "invasion." The mayor of Jackson added more than 100 new police to the city force and made arrangements to turn the fairgrounds into a makeshift prison. He also purchased 250 new shotguns, more paddy wagons and searchlight trucks and a new 13,000-pound steel armored personnel carrier with bulletproof windshields. Mississippi added 700 state troopers to its highway patrol.

At the week-long training course for the 800 student volunteers that took place in June on the campus of Western College for Women in Oxford, Ohio, SNCC veterans and Mississippi blacks told the young recruits what to expect. A black lawyer from Mississippi warned them that if a police officer stopped and arrested them even though they did nothing wrong, they should go to jail and not protest. He said Mississippi was not the place to conduct constitutional law classes for policemen, many of whom never went to school beyond the fifth grade.

On Sunday, June 21—the day after the first wave of about 200 students arrived in Mississippi—three young civil rights workers disappeared. Andrew Goodman, a 20-year-old white student at Queens College in New York City, was a summer volunteer, while the other two were CORE civil rights workers—James Chaney, a 21-year-old black plasterer from Meridian, Mississippi, and Michael Schwerner, a 24-year-old white man from Brooklyn, who had opened a CORE office in Meridian and set up a freedom school with his wife, Rita.

The three young men had driven to the town of Lawndale to investigate the burning of a black church. About three o'clock in the afternoon they were arrested near the town of Philadelphia, allegedly for speeding. They were put in jail and released later that night. Civil rights workers were required to telephone the project office at regular intervals, so when the three young men failed to call, the staff knew something was wrong. When they didn't come back that night, the Freedom Summer headquarters in Jackson informed the police, the FBI and the Justice Department.

Segregationists dismissed the disappearance of the three young men as a publicity stunt. The sheriff of the county where the young men disappeared suggested they were probably hiding out somewhere having a good laugh at all the fuss they had stirred up. Two days after their disappearance the station wagon they were driving was found buried in a swamp. As the national press reported the search for the missing young men, many feared the worst. "We are afraid they have been murdered," wrote one of the volunteers in a letter to his parents. "Under the circumstances, that is the only thing that could have happened to them."

President Johnson met with the parents of Goodman and Schwerner at the White House and dispatched 200 U.S. Navy personnel to Mississippi to drag the swamps and assist the Mississippi State Highway Patrol and the FBI in the search. On July 2, 1964, the president signed into law the Civil Rights Act that President Kennedy had submitted to Congress the previous year. However, the bill barring discrimination in public accommodations was of little help to the Freedom Summer project because it lacked a strong voter rights provision.

The disappearance of the civil rights workers failed to deter the work of the Freedom Summer volunteers, nor did the arrests, shootings and burnings of churches that served as "freedom schools." The students lived in shacks, church basements and empty stores with little more than a cot and electric plate and sometimes with little more than one meal a day. Some of the students picked vegetables and cotton to earn their keep.

The students taught reading, writing, math and black history and went door to door to register voters for the new Mississippi Freedom Democratic Party. Volunteer doctors set up clinics that provided free health care, and lawyers from the NAACP Legal Defense Fund, the National Lawyers Guild and the American Jewish Committee, assisted by students from the nation's leading law schools, ran legal clinics.

The most dramatic result of Freedom Summer and the one that received the most press coverage was the creation of the Mississippi Freedom Democratic Party (MFDP). Organized by SNCC to challenge the legitimacy and supremacy of Mississippi's all-white regular Democratic Party, the nation's first independent black-based political party quickly became a formidable force that captured the attention of the national Democratic Party.

When Freedom Summer volunteers convinced 80,000 blacks—and some whites as well—to join MFDP, SNCC sought the support of sympathetic Democrats around the country for their plan to have the MFDP confront the state's regular Democratic party at the Democratic National Convention in Atlantic City in August.

The party had managed to get the names of four MFDP candidates on the Mississippi Democratic primary ballot to be delegates to the convention, but all four lost because few blacks were registered to vote. Democrats in New York and Michigan supported MFDP's bid to represent Mississippi at the convention, and the liberal Americans for Democratic Action called for the seating of the integrated Mississippi Freedom Democratic Party in place of the all-white state Democratic delegation.

President Johnson backed the regular Mississippi Democratic Party because he feared losing the support of southern Democrats in the November general election. He worried that the Mississippi problem could divide the convention, detract from his renomination and endanger his reelection prospects against his conservative Republican opponent, Senator Barry Goldwater of Arizona.

In the meantime, in Mississippi on August 4—just 18 days before the Democratic National Convention was scheduled to begin—the FBI, acting on a tip from an informer, dug up the bodies of Chaney, Goodman and Schwerner on a farm outside Philadelphia. The bodies of the three civil rights workers had been riddled with .38-caliber bullets, and the fractured skull of James Cheney showed that he had been savagely beaten.

Nobody was arrested in the case until December when the FBI took into custody 21 Mississippi whites, including Deputy Sheriff Cecil Price, who had stopped and arrested the three, allegedly for speeding. Although a state court dropped the charges against the men, six of the accused were later convicted and sent to prison on federal charges of violating the civil rights of the murdered young men.

On August 6—two days after the discovery of the bodies once again focused the nation's attention on Mississippi—the 2,500 people attending the MFDP state convention in Jackson chose 64 blacks and four whites to serve as their delegates to the Democratic Convention. Hoping to convince the convention to seat their delegation in place of the regular party delegates, the MFDP took its case to the party's Credentials Committee, which was in charge of resolving seating disputes.

The powerful testimony of Fannie Lou Hamer, a sharecropper from Sunflower County, before the committee was carried on national television. Hamer spoke about the murders of Medgar Evers and Chaney, Goodman and Schwerner, the battle of James Meredith to enter the University of Mississippi and her own experiences in Mississippi where, for daring to try to register, the Ku Klux Klansmen pumped 16 bullets into her bedroom. She was also put in jail and beaten until there was no feeling in her arms. "Is this America," she asked the committee, "the land of the free and the home of the brave where we have to sleep with our telephones off the hooks because our lives be threatened daily because we want to live as decent human beings in America?"

The compromise the committee worked out—that the convention would seat the entire white Mississippi delegation if it swore to support the national ticket, and two MFDP delegates would be admitted to the convention as nonvoting delegates at large—pleased neither side. All but three members of the regular delegation left the convention and went back to Mississippi, refusing to support the national party. MFDP also refused to accept the committee's plan, even though many party liberals tried to talk

At the 1964 Democratic National Convention in Atlantic City, New Jersey, Fannie Lou Hamer, a former sharecropper and leader of the Mississippi Freedom Democratic Party (MFDP), told a national television audience about the injustices of segregation in her home state. *(Library of Congress)*

them into accepting the compromise by assuring them that more progress would be forthcoming in the future.

On the second night of the convention Fanny Lou Hamer and a group of MFDP delegates went to the convention floor with borrowed passes to sit in the vacant seats of the regulars who had walked out of the convention, but guards made them get out of the chairs and leave the convention. Convention managers then removed all but three of the chairs reserved for the Mississippi delegation and designated them for the three regular delegates who remained at the convention.

The next night MFDP delegates again managed to get into the convention with borrowed passes. Led by Fannie Lou Hamer, they stood in the space where the chairs had been and before the national television audience sang freedom songs, prayed and gave interviews that criticized the national party for the way it was treating Mississippi blacks. Although the MFDP never did get seated, its dramatic challenge to the state Democratic party marked the beginning of the end of exclusive white political control of the state. Fannie Lou Hamer said later that Freedom Summer changed the climate in Mississippi. "People who had never before tried, though they had always been anxious to do something, began moving." She said the more hopeful attitude was especially noticeable among young blacks. "To me it's one of the greatest things that ever happened in Mississippi. And it's a direct result of the Summer Project in 1964."

Freedom Summer was also important for the civil rights movement itself because it moved the struggle to a new level, beyond bus boycotts, freedom rides and sit-ins. Mississippi blacks demonstrated to the state and the nation that they wanted to vote, elect their representatives, and have a voice in government. They wanted the political power they were entitled to as American citizens. As James Bevel put it, black people were fighting for more than a seat at the lunch counter, they were now fighting for seats in the legislature.

*　　*　　*

The climactic battle of the voting rights struggle was fought in the small city of Selma in Dallas County in the middle of Alabama where only 156 of the 15,000 blacks of voting age in Selma were registered, compared to 65 percent of the 15,000 whites. The registration office in Selma was only open two days a month—on the first and third Mondays of the month. Registrars made a point of arriving late, leaving early and taking long lunch hours. For just showing up at the Dallas County courthouse to register, a black could be fired from his job. Those who dared try inevitably "failed" the test for not reading or interpreting complex sections of the state constitution to the registrar's satisfaction.

In 1963 SNCC workers tried to hold voter registration meetings to teach black people how to register, but Sheriff James Clark did all he could to obstruct the meetings and harass the people who came to them. He arrested SNCC workers who showed up at the courthouse. Local black ministers were afraid to let SNCC hold meetings in their churches for fear of having their churches burned down and their lives threatened.

After the passage of the 1964 Civil Rights Act, which mandated equal access to public accommodations, SNCC returned to Selma to try to integrate Selma's lunch counters and movie theaters. However, whites attacked them and Clark had them arrested for trespassing. When SNCC held a voter registration rally at the courthouse the next day, the police attacked the demonstrators with cattle prods. A circuit court judge then issued an order forbidding blacks to gather in public in groups of more than three people.

Several weeks after the civil rights movement achieved international recognition when Dr. Martin Luther King, Jr. was awarded the prestigious Nobel Peace Prize in Oslo, Norway in December 1964, King went to Selma. On January 2, 1965, King spoke to an overflow crowd of 700 people in Brown's Chapel of the African Methodist Episcopal Church about the right to vote. He told them that after they achieved that right, they would be able to send to the statehouse people who upheld justice, not people who stood in the doorways of universities to keep them out. The national and international media geared up for the major confrontation they expected in Selma over the issue of voter registration.

On Monday, January 18, 1965, the SCLC began its campaign of daily marches to the courthouse. Sheriff Clark was urged to avoid any violent confrontation that might become national news. Rather than arresting the blacks who went to the courthouse to register, the police ordered them to wait in an alley behind the building.

On Tuesday the demonstrators marched to the courthouse again, but this time when Sheriff Clark ordered them into the alley, they chose not to obey his orders. Clark lost his temper. When he grabbed Amelia Boynton by the coat and shoved her roughly down the street, the media caught the moment. He had her arrested along with 60 other blacks who shoved their way into the courthouse and refused to obey Clark's order to leave. Clark's strong-arm tactics made national news. The next morning newspapers around the country carried articles and editorials about the arrests and a dramatic Associated Press photograph of Sheriff Clark shoving Amelia Boynton down the street.

On Friday, 100 of Selma's black schoolteachers marched to the courthouse to protest the arrest of Amelia Boynton, and then went to Brown's Chapel for a rally. The participation of these highly respected middle-class teachers in the civil rights campaign encouraged other black groups to join the demonstrations—beauticians, undertakers, even schoolchildren inspired by the sight of their teachers demonstrating. Andrew Young of the SCLC called the Selma teachers' march the most important civil rights development since the Montgomery bus boycott.

SCLC's Selma strategy called for King to get arrested on Monday, February 1. That day, after addressing a group of 250 marchers in a church, King led them to the courthouse where they were all arrested, as were the 500 schoolchildren who followed them. By the end of the day several hundred more marchers were arrested, filling the city's jails. Television coverage of the mass arrests made America's unresolved race problem once again the focus of attention. Senator Jacob Javits of New York called the arrests "shocking," and a congressional delegation of 15 made plans to go to Selma to investigate.

While he was in jail Dr. King released a "Letter From a Selma Jail," which appeared in the *New York Times* on February 5. "Why are we in jail?" he asked. "Have you ever been required to answer 100 questions on government, some abstruse even to a political science specialist, merely to vote? Have you ever stood in line with over a hundred others and after waiting an entire day seen less than ten given the qualifying test? THIS IS SELMA, ALABAMA.

THERE ARE MORE NEGROES IN JAIL WITH ME THAN THERE ARE ON THE VOTING ROLLS."

At a nationally televised press conference, President Johnson said all Americans should be indignant whenever an American is denied the right to vote, and he pledged to work to see that that right is secured for all citizens. Two days later his press secretary announced that the president was going to send a voting rights proposal to Congress, but he gave no further details. After Dr. King was released from jail, he went to Washington to meet with the president. During their 15-minute meeting King urged the president to support a strong voting rights law.

Violence kept the spotlight on Selma. In the nearby town of Marion, angry whites, including state troopers and police, attacked people leaving a church after a rally. Troopers beat Jimmy Lee Jackson's grandfather and then killed Jackson when he tried to help. The angry mob, many of them police, beat dozens of others, including an NBC reporter. The story of police brutality in Marion became front-page news around the country. In Washington, Republican congressmen called for immediate action on a federal voting rights bill and criticized the Johnson administration for not moving fast enough.

In a sermon, SCLC's James Bevel proposed that civil rights demonstrators should march from Selma to Montgomery, the state capital, to make their case directly to Governor Wallace. Bevel had a flair for good ideas, having been the one who thought up the idea of having schoolchildren march in Birmingham. King liked Bevel's idea and got behind the plan for a 50-mile march along Route 80 to Montgomery to begin the following Sunday, March 7. When Governor Wallace heard about it, he announced that the state would not allow such a march, arguing that it would tie up traffic on the highway.

The day before the planned march 70 sympathetic local whites assembled on the steps of the Dallas County Courthouse in Selma to demonstrate their support. The minister who was chairman of the Concerned White Citizens of Alabama said they were there to show the country that there were white people in Alabama willing to speak out against the brutal way the police were breaking up peaceful demonstrations by American citizens who were exercising their constitutional rights.

On Sunday morning 600 people, headed by Hosea Williams of SCLC (Dr. King was in Atlanta conducting services at his church) and John Lewis, chairman of SNCC, lined up two by two and set out toward the Edmund Pettus Bridge that would take them to Route 80. At the bridge they were met by an army of Alabama state troopers dressed in blue uniforms and equipped with clubs and gas masks.

The major in charge of the state troops, John Cloud, ordered the marchers to stop and turn around. When Hosea Williams asked to have a word with him, Cloud said there was nothing to talk about and ordered his troopers to advance. They pushed and clubbed the front rows of the marchers and fired tear gas. Other troopers on horseback charged the marchers and clubbed them as they fled.

"I was terrified," said one of the youngest members of the march, 8-year-old Sheyann Webb. "I saw those horsemen coming toward me and they had those awful masks on; they rode right through the cloud of tear gas. Some of them had clubs, others had ropes, or whips, which they swung about them like they were driving cattle."

Television coverage of the charge interrupted regular network programming. The vivid footage of state troopers beating defenseless civilians shocked and enraged the public. In Atlanta, King sent telegrams to clergymen across the country inviting them to come to Selma for a ministers' march to Montgomery on Tuesday.

On Monday—the day after "Bloody Sunday," as it came to be called—SCLC asked U.S. District Court Judge Frank Johnson to prevent Governor Wallace from interfering with the march. Judge Johnson promised he would hold a hearing on the matter later in the week, but he ordered the march not to take place until after the hearing. That put Dr. King in a dilemma. He had to choose between going ahead with the march in defiance of the federal court order or canceling the march that hundreds of people from all over the country were coming to join. King decided to go ahead with the march with a promise from the Justice Department that if he turned the march back before it reached the police line, there would be no violence.

On Tuesday after addressing the people packed into Brown's Chapel, King led 1,500 marchers out of the church and down the street toward the bridge. The Alabama state troopers were waiting at the same place, and once again the major in charge ordered the marchers to turn back. After the marchers sang "We Shall Overcome," Dr. King knelt down in front of the state troopers and asked Abernathy to lead them in prayer.

Then to everybody's surprise Dr. King stood up, turned and led the marchers back to the church. The marchers were confused, and many were upset that King had backed down. King felt they had made their point and another round of police brutality was averted. Besides, the federal judge would be making his ruling about the legality of the march in a couple of days. When King asked those who had come to Selma from other places to stay on for a few more days, many did.

That night in Selma a group of whites assaulted the Reverend James Reeb, a young white Unitarian minister, outside a black restaurant where a group of white ministers had gone to eat after having been advised not to eat in the white downtown area. The attack on Reeb, who died two days later, angered the nation, causing demonstrations in many cities.

On Monday night—March 15, 1965—President Johnson presented his proposal for a Voting Rights Act to a joint session of Congress. "I speak tonight for the dignity of man and the destiny of democracy," he said in his Southern drawl to Congress and the 70 million Americans watching on television. "At times history and fate meet at a single time in a single place to shape a turning point in man's unending search for freedom. So it was at Lexington and Concord. So it was a century ago at Appomattox. So it was last week in Selma, Alabama."

"The cause of the Negro must be our cause, too," he told the nation. "Because it's not just Negroes, but it's really all of us who must overcome the crippling legacy of bigotry and injustice. And we shall overcome. We *shall* overcome!" These last words, the refrain of the black freedom song that had become the anthem of the civil rights movement, the president spoke slowly and with great feeling.

The president's speech to Congress was the climax of a decade of struggle for equal justice. The movement to end discrimination was no longer the goal of just black Americans and the civil rights movement. Racial justice was now a national priority, supported by the majority of white Americans and backed by the full weight of the federal government. By the end of the speech most congressmen were ready to pass a law that would finally end the disgrace of American citizens being denied the right to vote. If the March on Washington was the end of the beginning of the struggle, Selma was the beginning of the end.

The day after the president's speech, Judge Johnson announced that his careful review of the record of Alabama lawmen over the preceding two months convinced him of the presence of "an almost continuous pattern of harassment, intimidation, coercion, threatening conduct and, sometimes, brutal mistreatment" in order to prevent blacks "from exercising their rights of citizenship, particularly the right to register to vote and the right to demonstrate peaceably for the purpose of protesting discriminatory practices." He ruled that the plaintiffs—the SCLC—had the legal and constitutional right to march from Selma to Montgomery.

When Governor Wallace announced that the state of Alabama could not protect the march nor guarantee the safety of the marchers, President Johnson federalized the Alabama National Guard and dispatched 2,000 U.S. troops, 100 FBI agents and 100 federal marshals to Alabama to protect the march.

The march finally took place on Sunday, March 21. Four thousand marchers, black and white, assembled at Brown's Chapel. Joining Dr. King as leaders of the march were Ralph Bunche, the black American diplomat and winner of the Nobel Peace Prize, and Rabbi Abraham Heschel of the Jewish Theological Seminary. As the marchers set off, angry whites lined the route to shout and jeer. However, the troops protected the marchers from attack and searched for snipers.

For five days the Selma-to-Montgomery march was front-page news around the world. Volunteers from the march headquarters in Selma drove food and supplies to the marchers, who slept in tents along the way at night. The symbolism of the march could not have been more dramatic: the civil rights army marching toward Montgomery and the Alabama state capitol with its

Alabama state troopers line up in front of the state capitol in
Montgomery, with the state and Confederate flags flying
overhead. They are waiting for the civil rights march that
began in Selma on March 21 and reached the capital on
March 25, 1965. *(Photographs and Prints Division/Schomburg
Center for Research in Black Culture–New York Public Library/Astor,
Lenox and Tilden Foundations)*

Confederate flag flying overhead. In the meantime, the Voting Rights Act was making its way through Congress.

On Thursday, March 25, the marchers—now 25,000 strong—reached Montgomery. As the march passed the Dexter Avenue Baptist Church, which had been Dr. King's church during the Montgomery bus boycott, Coretta Scott King reflected on how far the civil rights movement had come in ten years. The bus boycott had involved only blacks, but the march from Selma to Montgomery included many white people, including ministers, rabbis, priests and nuns from all parts of the country.

National television recorded the drama of Martin Luther King, Jr. leading the march through the streets of Montgomery to the state capitol with the other leaders and heroes of the civil rights struggle, including Rosa Parks, who had started it all ten years earlier.

After Dr. King spoke to the thousands of civil rights marchers in front of the state capitol, concluding his speech with the words of "The Battle Hymn of the Republic," eight march leaders presented a petition to a representative of Governor Wallace, who was holed up in his office in the capitol behind closed venetian blinds. The petition asked the governor to remove all obstacles that prevented blacks from registering to vote in the state of Alabama.

That night when Viola Liuzzo, a white volunteer from Detroit, was killed on Route 80 by four members of the Ku Klux Klan, the nation was again horrified and more insistent that Congress pass the Voting Rights Act. Five weeks later the Senate passed the bill 77 to 19, followed by the House. It then went to the president for his signature.

On August 6, 1965, President Johnson signed the Voting Rights Act into law in the presence of Martin Luther King, Rosa Parks and other heroes of the civil rights movement in the President's Room off the Capitol Rotunda, where 104 years earlier Abraham Lincoln had signed the Emancipation Proclamation. The president called the Voting Rights Act "one of the most monumental laws in the entire history of American freedom."

By taking registration out of the hands of local segregationists and putting it in the hands of federal officials, black Americans gained what President Johnson called "the most powerful instru-

A federal official registers a woman to vote in Canton, Mississippi in August 1965. After President Lyndon Johnson signed the 1965 Voting Rights Act, federal registrars helped register many thousands of first-time black voters in the South. *(Library of Congress)*

ment ever devised by man for breaking down injustice and destroying the terrible walls which imprison men because they are different from other men."

As blacks began registering in large numbers, they started electing their own representatives—sheriffs, mayors, state legislators and members of Congress. One year after the Voting Rights Act was passed, the 9,000 newly registered black voters of Dallas County voted Sheriff Jim Clark out of office. The 1965 Voting Rights Act sounded the death knell for segregation in the South.

CHAPTER SIX NOTES

page 76   "national sentiments . . . prominent families." **Civil Rights**, p. 103.

page 78   "We are afraid . . . to them." **Road**, p. 111.

page 80   "Is this America . . . in America?" *Kay Mills*, **This Little Light of Mine: The Life of Fannie Lou Hamer**. New York, Plume, 1994, p. 121.

page 82   "People . . . To me . . . in 1964." **Eyes**, p. 249.

pages 84–85 "Why are we in jail? . . . VOTING ROLLS." Quoted in **Bearing**, p. 386.

page 86   "I was terrified . . . driving cattle." Quoted in **Civil Rights**, p. 131.

page 87   "I speak tonight . . . The cause of the Negro . . . We *shall* overcome." Quoted in **Road**, p. 2.

page 88   "an almost continuous . . . mistreatment" and "from exercising . . . discriminatory practices." Quoted in **Bearing**, p. 410.

pages 90–92 "one of the most . . . freedom" and "the most powerful . . . other men." Quoted in **Eyes**, p. 285.

CHAPTER **Seven**

A MORE MILITANT TONE
Malcolm X, Black Power and Urban Unrest

Selma turned out to be the last great gathering of the unified civil rights movement. After it was over a more militant tone took hold among many of its younger members. Although SNCC and other young activists still believed in the value of nonviolence, some students and young activists were turning to more confrontational tactics to protest segregation and defend themselves against racial violence.

As the movement expanded and broadened its base, it picked up support from people from different backgrounds, age groups, social classes and parts of the country. The civil rights movement could no longer speak with a single voice or present a united front. A growing number of young blacks in the urban ghettos were more drawn to the message of black pride and self-defense than to the message of nonviolence and integration advocated by Dr. King and the southern-based civil rights movement. They were more interested in strengthening the black community than in what some saw as denying their blackness in order to advance in the white world.

White interest and involvement began to fade after passage of the 1965 Voting Rights Act gave blacks the last great civil right—the right to vote. Some whites felt less welcome in the movement when the emphasis of young black activists shifted from "freedom now" to "black power." Furthermore, many young whites soon redirected their idealism and energy to protesting the escalating war in Vietnam.

The division between SNCC activists and the older, more established groups that divided the civil rights movement after Selma first appeared back in August 1963, behind the scenes at the March on Washington over the speech by John Lewis of SNCC.

The day before the march, after the scheduled speakers submitted copies of their prepared speeches to the march organizing committee, there were complaints that the speech to be delivered by Lewis was too inflammatory. Written by several SNCC members, the speech criticized the Kennedy civil rights bill and had a decidedly militant tone.

One section of the speech said, "We will march through the South, through the heart of Dixie, the way Sherman did. We shall pursue our own 'scorched earth' policy and burn Jim Crow to the ground—nonviolently. We shall crack the South into a thousand pieces and put them back together in the image of democracy." Archbishop Patrick O'Boyle of Washington, who was scheduled to give the invocation, objected to the violent tone of the language, as did Walter Reuther and some of the other march leaders.

Lewis defended his speech and refused to compromise, so the controversy continued right up to the time the speeches were scheduled to begin. Archbishop O'Boyle threatened to walk off the podium if the speech wasn't changed. The argument backstage got so heated that Rustin ordered the National Anthem to be played over the loudspeakers. To stall for more time he had Dr. Ralph Bunche and the Reverend Fred Shuttlesworth make some remarks while Randolph, King and Eugene Carson Blake of the National Council of Churches worked on Lewis backstage. "John, I know you as well as anybody," said King. "That doesn't *sound* like you." Lewis finally agreed to tone down some but not all of his speech.

✳   ✳   ✳

The man most responsible for the more radical tone of young SNCC activists and other students was Malcolm X, the Black Muslim leader from New York who preached black nationalism. Unlike most of the college-educated, middle-class, theology-trained black leaders of the civil rights movement, Malcolm X was the product of northern ghetto life who had served time in prison, where he converted to Islam. He disagreed strongly with the nonviolent strategy of the civil rights movement and its goal of integration into the white mainstream. By the 1960s he had become a powerful voice for a more radical approach to the race problem in America.

Malcolm X was born Malcolm Little in Omaha, Nebraska on May 19, 1925. He was the fourth of eight children born to Earl and Louise Little. Earl Little was a traveling preacher and active recruiter for the Universal Negro Improvement Association, a black nationalist organization founded by Marcus Garvey.

Malcolm's father became the target of several attacks by the Ku Klux Klan, the southern-based white supremacist group. One night several weeks before Malcolm's birth, white-robed Klansmen on horses surrounded the Little house with the intention of lynching Reverend Little. When the visibly pregnant Louise Little went out and told them her husband was away on business, they smashed the windows of the house with rifle butts and told Louise Little to tell her husband to get out of town.

Shortly after the attack the Littles did move north, first to Milwaukee, Wisconsin, then Lansing, Michigan. Earl Little hoped that in Lansing he could put down roots and establish a strong black organization far from the racial bigotry he had experienced farther south. But when Malcolm was four years old night riders struck again. They set fire to the Little home, forcing the Littles to move once more—this time to the nearby town of East Lansing. In 1931 Malcolm's father left home one night never to return. They found his body in downtown East Lansing with his head beaten in. His murderers were never found.

The death of Earl Little left the family in bad shape during the worst years of the Depression. When the state welfare authorities committed Malcolm's mother to a mental hospital, they made the Little children wards of the state. When Malcolm was 13 he was expelled from school and sent to a juvenile detention center in Mason, Michigan.

He attended the junior high school in Mason, where he was popular and got good grades. However, a visit to his half-sister Ella in Roxbury, a largely black district in Boston, convinced him he wanted to live with other blacks in a big city. Malcolm left

After his conversion to the Black Muslim religion, Malcolm X
became an outspoken and dynamic black leader whose
message of militant black nationalism appealed to large
numbers of blacks. *(Library of Congress)*

school as soon as he could and moved to Boston, where he set out to live a life filled with money, women and excitement. He sold sandwiches on the Yankee Clipper passenger train that traveled between Boston and New York, but he was fired after he was accused of using drugs and alcohol and being rude to passengers.

He then moved to Harlem in New York in December 1941 and immediately fell in love with its nightlife. The 17-year-old got a job at a restaurant that was a meeting place for street hustlers and members of the Harlem underworld, and soon Malcolm was part of that scene, peddling drugs and getting prostitutes for U.S. servicemen who came to Harlem looking for excitement before they shipped out overseas. "Everybody in Harlem needed some kind of hustle to survive," he later said, "and needed to stay high in some way to forget what they had to do to survive."

In August 1943, after a race riot sparked by a fight between a white policeman and a black soldier left five people dead and 400 wounded and devastated Harlem's business district, Harlem became poorer and unemployment soared as whites stopped visiting Harlem's theaters and nightclubs. Malcolm survived by becoming a numbers runner, but after close scrapes with mobsters who controlled the illegal lottery game almost cost him his life, he left Harlem and returned to Roxbury.

There he became involved with gambling and numbers operations and operated a burglary ring with a friend until 1945, when the police uncovered the ring and arrested him. A judge sentenced him to a 10-year prison term. In February 1946, at age 20, he entered Boston's Charlestown State Prison to serve his sentence.

At first he had to be put in solitary confinement for his destructive outbursts, but then he settled down and began attending classes at the prison. His decision to educate himself proved to be one of the major turning points in his life. After he was transferred to Norfolk Prison, a more modern facility, his brothers and sisters wrote to him to encourage him to learn about the Nation of Islam, a Black Muslim religious group headed by Elijah Muhammad, that tried to help blacks reclaim their racial identity and cultural heritage that centuries of slavery and oppression had destroyed. Elijah Muhammed preached that blacks were superior to whites and were fated to rule the world. Hearing about their belief in the supremacy of the black race revived a sense of pride Malcolm had not felt since he attended meetings of the Universal Negro Improvement Association with his father.

After his brother Reginald visited him in prison and his other Black Muslim siblings sent him letters urging him to join the Nation of Islam, Malcolm underwent a conversion in 1949 that radically changed his life and set him on his future course. At the urging of his brothers and sisters, Malcolm wrote to Elijah Muhammad, who answered him promptly, welcoming him to the community of Islam. Following a custom of the Black Muslims, 24-year-old Malcolm Little dropped his surname and replaced it with the letter X. Black Muslims believed that shedding the name given by a slave master was an important step in freeing oneself from the slave mentality encouraged by the white world.

Malcolm X set out to expand his self-discipline and knowledge and followed strict Islamic rules and rituals. Every day he copied a page of the dictionary to improve his handwriting, and he wrote letters to his former underworld friends urging them to follow his example. He also wrote many letters to government officials about the need for racial justice. At the Norfolk Prison library Malcolm X devoured books on history, religion, philosophy, archaeology, science and revolutionary politics.

As he grew in knowledge and self-confidence, he became a zealous, disciplined spokesman for Islam. His improved behavior impressed the prison authorities so much they released him from prison in 1952 at the age of 27, after he had served six years of his 10-year sentence.

After his release he went to Detroit to work and live with his brother Wilfred. While working as a furniture salesman in the store his brother managed, Malcolm X joined and became an active participant in Detroit's Nation of Islam community. On fire with his new faith, he spread the teachings of the Nation of Islam at every opportunity and visited Elijah Muhammad in Chicago to tell him he was willing to spread the message in any way he could.

Back in Detroit, Malcolm X searched tirelessly for converts on street corners and in bars and pool halls. Although many thought he was something of an oddball, others were drawn to his message about black pride and about how the Islamic god Allah was soon going to banish the white race from the face of the earth. Before long, Malcolm X singlehandedly tripled the membership of the Detroit temple.

Recognizing the young man's sincerity, charisma and effectiveness, Elijah Muhammad sent him to other cities to recruit new members. Soon Malcolm X was playing a central role in the building of the Nation of Islam into a powerful national organization. His blistering sermons urged blacks to liberate themselves from their dependence on "white slavemasters." We never can win freedom and justice and equality, he told his listeners, until we do something for ourselves. In 1953 Elijah Muhammad sent him to Boston to organize a Black Muslim temple, and then to Philadelphia to do the same.

As a reward for his hard work, Malcolm X was appointed head of Temple Number Seven in Harlem. Only ten years after he had been one of Harlem's most troubled street hustlers, he was back as the voice of Allah calling for revolution in the largest black community in America.

With his customary energy he increased membership in the temple and traveled around the country preaching in other cities. He also helped organize Nation of Islam rallies and conventions in major cities around the country. By the late 1950s, thanks in part to Malcolm X's zeal, the Nation of Islam had become a powerful force in the nation's largest cities and a force to be reckoned with in America.

While the civil rights movement was conducting its nonviolent campaigns in the South, Malcolm X was inspiring blacks in northern ghettos with a message of another kind. Maintaining that blacks could not afford to wait patiently for racial justice, he called for a black revolution against the white power structure. He criticized the nonviolent tactics of the civil rights movement that asked black people to put their bodies and in some cases their lives on the line. He opposed the goal of integration and called on blacks to create their own society. He preached that blacks should not turn the other cheek to those who abuse them, but rather they should defend themselves against violence "by any means necessary."

While many black leaders saw the early civil rights victories as a hopeful sign of progress, Malcolm X refused to be optimistic about race relations in America. He said the black masses were living "a nightmare" and black people wanted their own society in a land of their own. Like his father, Malcolm dreamed of a black revolution that would alter dramatically the relationship between the races. He believed that only the threat of a massive black uprising would pressure the U.S. government to get serious about major racial reform.

Malcolm X told his listeners at rallies in Harlem and other northern cities that as long as blacks lived under white domination, they would never know peace or justice. He said the only solution to the race problem was for black people to form their own nation, either in the United States or in Africa.

As sweeping changes in the country's racial attitudes failed to materialize in the 1960s, despite the victories of the civil rights movement, more and more young blacks, especially those trapped in northern ghettos, agreed with Malcolm X that nonviolent protests were not getting results fast enough. Young urban blacks flocked to hear him speak.

Malcolm X considered himself a champion of black liberation, but his critics accused him of being a violent rabble-rouser, hatemonger, revolutionary and extremist. "Yes, I'm an extremist," he admitted. "The black race here in North America is in extremely bad condition." He wanted to free black people from what he regarded as the misguided policies of moderate black leaders, whom he described as men with black bodies and white heads.

In 1962 Elijah Muhammed, who was in poor health, appointed Malcolm X national minister of the Nation of Islam, thus making him acting prime minister of the organization and heir apparent to succeed Elijah Muhammed. However, the appointment made other Black Muslims jealous, and soon Malcolm X had reason to believe that his rivals were trying to turn Elijah Muhammad against him. Malcolm's name and picture appeared less frequently in the Black Muslim newspaper *Muhammad Speaks*, and Muhammad soon ordered him not to accept invitations to appear on national television.

In the meantime, Malcolm X's fresh, powerful voice on behalf of militant black resistance put him at odds with mainstream black leaders. He called the 1963 March on Washington the "farce on Washington" because he claimed that it only diverted attention away from the country's racial problems. "I don't believe we're going to overcome by singing," he told reporters. "If you're going to get yourself a .45 and start singing 'We Shall Overcome,' I'm with you."

By the end of 1963 he was deeply involved in a political power struggle within the Nation of Islam. When he heard rumors that Elijah Muhammed had fathered four children by two of his secretaries, who were serving him with paternity suits, Malcolm X found his faith shaken, since adultery is a serious violation of Muslim ethics. When Malcolm X asked Muhammad directly about the matter, instead of denying the accusations, the older man compared himself to David and Noah, who also had moral lapses. Malcolm X was disappointed and felt estranged from his former idol.

After President John Kennedy was assassinated on November 22, 1963, Malcolm X said the shooting was a case of "the chickens coming home to roost," meaning that whites were paying the price for the climate of hatred and violence they had created in America. His comment caused an uproar, and Muhammad used the occasion to suspend him from his national duties for 90 days. Malcolm X was shaken when he learned that some Black Muslims were plotting to kill him for his alleged rebellion against Muhammed.

In January 1964 Muhammed summoned Malcolm X to Chicago to face accusations by his rivals that he was planning a rebellion. After their talk Muhammed ordered him to go back to New York and put out the fire he had started. When a member of his temple in New York informed Malcolm X that the Nation's Chicago headquarters had sent out word that he be killed, he knew only one man could have given the order—Elijah Muhammad.

Malcolm X continued to dismiss the achievements of the civil rights movement. After Congress passed the 1964 Civil Rights Act, he said the new laws were little more than window dressing. "You don't stick a knife in a man's back nine inches and pull it out six inches and say you're making progress." He pointed to recent outbreaks of racial violence in northern cities as evidence that the ghettos were about to explode.

In March 1964, at a crowded press conference, Malcolm X announced that he was leaving the Nation of Islam to found an organization called Muslim Mosque, Incorporated. He said Muslim Mosque would be a revolutionary group whose goal was to eliminate the political oppression, economic exploitation and social degradation suffered by 22 million black Americans every day. The leaders of the Nation of Islam condemned him, and Black Muslim newspapers branded him a hypocrite and traitor.

Malcolm's split with the Nation of Islam seemed to broaden his horizons. He became more interested in learning about the orthodox Islam practiced in the Middle East, and even took religious instruction and studied the Koran with an Egyptian professor in New York.

In the spring of 1964 he made the pilgrimage, or *hajj*, to the holy city of Mecca in Saudi Arabia. He was deeply moved by the experience and the spirit of harmony and understanding he found among people of all races. He said in his autobiography, "Never have I witnessed such sincere hospitality and the overwhelming spirit of true brotherhood . . . I have been utterly speechless and spellbound by the graciousness I see displayed all around me by people *of all colors.*"

Before leaving Mecca, Malcolm X took as his Islamic name El-Hajj Malik El-Shabazz. On his way back he visited Lebanon, Nigeria, Ghana and Algeria. When he addressed the parliament of Ghana at the invitation of President Kwame Nkrumah, he linked the struggle of black African nations for freedom and independence to that of blacks in America. He declared that racism, poverty, and oppression had common roots throughout the world and called his new international perspective "global black thinking."

Upon his return to the United States he called on blacks of all nations to unite in a revolutionary movement that would sweep away all vestiges of racial oppression. However, he also moderated some of his earlier views. He indicated his willingness to work with the civil rights movement and even with those he had formerly called "white devils." "I can get along with white people who can get along with me," he said.

By late 1964 Malcolm X had even more reason to fear for his safety. Members of the Nation of Islam attacked his associates, and by December Malcolm X himself was receiving death threats both at home and at his office. Besides the Nation of Islam, federal government agents were keeping close watch on him. Feeling surrounded by his enemies, Malcolm X suspected a conspiracy was in the works to kill him.

On February 4, 1965, Malcolm X made a rare appearance at a civil rights event when at the invitation of SNCC he went to Selma during the voter registration campaign and spoke at a rally in Brown's Chapel. With King in jail at the time some SCLC leaders worried that Malcolm X might incite some of the local people to strike out on their own and threaten King's control of the movement.

With Coretta Scott King in the audience, Malcolm X told the capacity crowd that white people should be grateful that Dr. King was keeping blacks in check with his message of nonviolence when other black leaders like himself believed that black people should strike back at those who attack them. If white people realize what the alternative is, he said, perhaps they will be more willing to hear Dr. King.

Nine days later—on the night of February 13—Malcolm X's home in East Elmhurst, New York was firebombed. He and his family were asleep when suddenly gasoline firebombs crashed through the living room window. Malcolm managed to get his wife and four daughters out of the house just before it went up in flames.

The end came on February 21, 1965, when Malcolm X went to the Audubon Ballroom for his weekly meeting with the Harlem community. When he got to the stage to begin the meeting, three men pulled out their guns and riddled him with bullets in front of his wife and daughters. His aides rushed him to the hospital emergency room, but it was too late. Malcolm X was dead at the age of 39.

Police detectives suspected the killing was the work of the Nation of Islam, but they found no real proof. Three men were convicted, but the identity of the people who arranged the assassination remains a mystery to this day.

The Muslim Mosque dissolved shortly after Malcolm X's death, but black voices inside and outside the Nation of Islam continued to call for a black revolution and radical transformation of American society.

Although Malcolm X's voice was stilled, the force of his words and spirit continued to influence SNCC members and other young black activists as well as many young urban blacks. Later, with the fragmentation of the civil rights movement in the 1970s and its ebbing in the 1980s, Malcolm X's spirit and message gained new adherents in the black community. Today his legacy continues to exert a powerful influence.

*　　*　　*

Within the civil rights movement itself, Malcolm X's influence was apparent in the mid-1960s when at least two major civil rights groups—SNCC and CORE—and many local ones shifted their allegiance from an ideology of nonviolent protest and passive resistance to one of black power and self-defense.

SNCC displayed its more radical tone and direction immediately after Selma when it targeted poverty-stricken Lowndes County in Alabama, which SNCC workers had seen firsthand on the march from Selma to Montgomery. The county was one of the poorest in the nation, and its blacks were among the most oppressed anywhere. The local aristocracy—a cluster of white families that owned 90 percent of the land—lived comfortably in their big houses, while most of the blacks in the county lived below the poverty line down dirt roads in unpainted shacks without water, heat, electricity, plumbing and glass windows.

Nowhere were disenfranchisement and the denial of political rights more blatant than in Lowndes County. The motto of the Alabama Democratic Party which controlled the county was "white supremacy." Although the 12,000 blacks who lived in the county made up 80 percent of its population, by the beginning of 1965 not a single black person had been allowed to register.

Whites kept blacks from registering by economic and physical intimidation. The Ku Klux Klan was active throughout the county, and Klan crosses were manufactured and stockpiled in the county's largest town. The local Klan made news the night of the Selma-to-Montgomery march when four of their number killed Viola Liuzzo, a white civil rights volunteer from Detroit.

The day after the shooting became front-page news around the country, SNCC leader Stokely Carmichael slipped into Lowndes County to begin the organization's campaign to organize a black political power base outside the Democratic Party, something SNCC had been planning for months, after the Democratic convention refused to seat the Mississippi Freedom Party the previous summer.

Shortly before the Selma-to-Montgomery march when John Hulett succeeded in registering he became the first black person to register to vote in Lowndes County since Reconstruction. Nonetheless, despite intense efforts by Hulett and SNCC activists, only 250 more blacks were registered by August because of white intimidation tactics. Whites fired any black employees and drove off the land any sharecroppers who attempted to register. To make it even harder for the blacks to register, county officials changed the place of registration without informing blacks or simply closed the office.

However, after President Lyndon Johnson signed the Voting Rights Act, the federal government sent a registrar to Lowndes to enforce the new law. As blacks registered in greater numbers, whites in the county became more hostile. On August 20, 1965, a part-time deputy sheriff, Tom Coleman, shot two civil rights workers—Jonathan Daniels, an Episcopalian theology student from Cambridge, Massachusetts, and Father Richard Morrisroe, a Catholic priest—after they were released from jail. Daniels died, but Morrisroe survived. Coleman was later tried for the killing, but an all-white jury acquitted him.

When SNCC found out that Alabama law permitted the formation of new political parties at the county level, they organized the Lowndes County Freedom Organization (LCFO) and chose a black panther as the party symbol. Despite white intimidation and obstruction, LCFO held its first political convention in the county, and in the Alabama primary, 900 of the 2,000 newly registered blacks in Lowndes County voted for "Black Panther" party candidates.

The image of the snarling black panther that symbolized the surge of black political consciousness in Lowndes County spread across the country. In Oakland, California, the black panther became the symbol of a new Black Panther party. When Stokely Carmichael defeated John Lewis for the chairmanship of SNCC in May 1966, the student organization adopted an even more radical tone and direction. Back in Alabama, Lowndes County was changed forever after blacks were allowed to register and vote. In

1970, John Hulett, who had been denied the right to vote most of his life, was elected sheriff of the county.

When Carmichael called for "black power" on the Meredith march of 1966, it quickly became the rallying cry of young blacks across the country. James Meredith had reemerged in the news when he set out on June 5, 1966, on his personal "march against fear" from Memphis, Tennessee to Jackson, Mississippi. The purpose of his walk was to encourage blacks in his home state of Mississippi to register and vote. However, on the second day of his journey a white man hiding along the route shot him. After Meredith was hospitalized, Martin Luther King, Jr., Stokely Carmichael and other civil rights leaders went to Memphis to visit him. Meredith survived the attack after emergency surgery, but he was in no shape to continue the march. Although the civil rights leaders disagreed about nonviolence and allowing whites to participate, they continued the Meredith march.

It was in Greenwood, Mississippi where Stokely Carmichael first called for "black power," and it immediately became a competing slogan to the traditional "freedom now" of the followers of Dr. King's southern-based civil rights movement. The national media, which were covering the march, immediately picked up the new term and publicized it to the rest of the country. Almost at once there was a heated debate within the civil rights movement and the country about the meaning and significance of black power. Many civil rights supporters worried it signaled a significant shift away from nonviolence and the goal of integration toward the more militant tone and goals of Malcolm X's black nationalism.

By June 24 James Meredith was well enough to rejoin the marchers in the town of Canton, allowing him to finish the march he started by leading it into Jackson on June 26—three weeks after he began. As a result of this effort, 4,000 additional blacks registered in Mississippi, and the electrifying new phrase—"black power"—became an instant rallying cry for many young blacks around the country and a source of worry for many whites anxious about rising racial tensions in the nation's cities.

One of the major sources of racial tension in cities had always been friction caused by the presence of white police in black neighborhoods. Black reaction to police actions was often the

A mason cleans bricks from the rubble of destroyed stores on 103d Street after the 1965 riot in the Watts section of Los Angeles, California. *(Library of Congress)*

spark that set off urban riots. The shooting of a 15-year-old boy by an off-duty police lieutenant triggered the 1964 Harlem riot, while the spark that set off the riot in the Watts section of Los Angeles in 1965 was the arrest of a young black driver by the highway patrol. Such explosions were usually the culmination of many years of grievances among blacks against the white police. Black residents perceived the patrol cars carrying heavily armed white police through their neighborhoods as more of a threat than a protection. For many blacks, the ghettos in which they lived felt like occupied colonies controlled and policed by the white power structure.

In Oakland, California, growing antagonism toward the white police department led two young black men, Huey Newton and Bobby Seale, to found a new political party they called the Black Panther Party for Self-Defense. Organized in October 1966 and inspired in part by the success of the Lowndes County Freedom Organization in Alabama, the Black Panthers monitored the Oakland police and carried guns, which at the time were legal in

California if they were not concealed. The party's 10-point program included an immediate end to police brutality, full employment and decent housing for blacks, the teaching of black history and black juries for trials involving black defendants.

The Black Panthers dressed distinctively—black leather jackets, black pants, blue shirts and black berets—as they patrolled black neighborhoods with their guns, tape recorders and law books, which they used to advise blacks of their legal rights when they were stopped by the police. Black Panthers also advised welfare recipients about their rights, taught black history courses and protested rent evictions. The image of young black men carrying guns on the streets of American cities was a shock to most white Americans.

To take the guns out of the hands of the Black Panthers, the California state legislature passed a law in July 1967 that made it illegal to carry loaded firearms in public. In late October, after an early morning shoot-out left one police officer dead and another seriously wounded, Huey Newton, who himself had four bullet wounds in his stomach, was charged with murder.

The Black Panther Party, which soon had chapters in 25 cities despite intense efforts by the FBI to disrupt their activities, organized dozens of "Free Huey" rallies. Newton was convicted of voluntary manslaughter and served almost two years of his sentence before the California State Court of Appeals unanimously reversed his conviction.

The summer of 1967 revealed to America just how serious inner-city problems were when disorders broke out in nearly 150 cities. The worst American riot since the 1965 Watts uprising raged in Newark from July 12 through July 17, and left 26 dead; the riot which followed a week later in Detroit was even worse in terms of lives lost and property destroyed.

The Detroit death toll after five days was 41, with estimates of the injured ranging between 300 and 600, including 85 police. More than 4,000 people were arrested, and 5,000 were left homeless. Fire damaged close to 700 buildings, and property losses reached $45 million. One week after the riot started the last of 4,700 National Guard paratroopers who had been ordered into the ghetto to restore order left the city. Two days later a government

A Black Panther convention banner on display at the Lincoln Memorial, Washington, D.C., in June, 1970. *(Library of Congress)*

spokesman declared that law and order had been restored in Detroit.

After Selma, the turmoil in the nation's cities and the economic plight of black Americans generally became the central focus of the increasingly multi-faceted civil rights movement. In the last half of the 1960s as the earlier, specific objectives of desegregation and voting rights were replaced by broader economic and political goals, the fight for jobs, housing and health care became the main issues of the movement.

CHAPTER SEVEN NOTES

page 94   "We will march . . . image of democracy." **Parting**, pp. 873–874.

page 94   "John, I know . . . like you." **Parting**, p. 879.

page 97   "Everybody in Harlem . . . survive." *Jack Rummel.* **Malcolm X**. New York: Chelsea House, 1989, p. 39.

page 100   "Yes . . . bad condition." **X**, p. 83.

page 100   "farce on Washington" *Walter Dean Myers*, **Malcolm X: By Any Means Necessary**. New York: Scholastic, 1993, p. 130.

pages 100– "I don't believe . . . with you." **X**, p. 88.
101

page 101   "the chickens coming home to roost" **Malcolm X, By Any Means Necessary** (2nd ed.). New York: Pathfinder, 1992, p. ix.

page 101   "You don't stick a knife . . . making progress." **X**, p. 88.

page 102   "Never have I . . . *of all colors.*" *Malcolm X,* **The Autobiography of Malcolm X**. New York: Ballantine, 1992, pp. 370–371.

CHAPTER Eight

NEW DIRECTIONS
The Final King Years and Beyond

After passage of the 1965 Voting Rights Act, Martin Luther King, Jr. and his colleagues in the Southern Christian Leadership Conference concluded that it was not enough to change laws. The lives of blacks had to change too. Discontent with the poverty and powerlessness of ghetto life was stirring in the nation's cities, as the rhetoric of President Johnson's Great Society and War on Poverty programs was raising expectations that were not being met.

In 1966 Martin Luther King, Jr. took his southern-based civil rights campaign north to Chicago. "I am appalled that some people feel that the civil rights struggle is over because we have a 1964 civil rights bill with ten titles and a voting rights bill," he had said on an earlier tour of northern cities. "Over and over again people ask, What else do you want? They feel that everything is all right. Well, let them look around at our big cities."

However, to many blacks in the North, King's message of nonviolence seemed out of step with the tenor of the times. The message of Malcolm X and the Black Panthers seemed more in keeping with the angry, frustrated mood in the ghettos. When Dr. King went to Los Angeles after the Watts riot in 1965, he was booed and heckled. New York Congressman Adam Clayton Powell, Jr. of Harlem let him know in no uncertain terms he would not be welcome in his district. When he visited Philadelphia the city's black leaders greeted him reluctantly.

Only when activists in Chicago's Coordinating Council of Community Organizations (CCCO) felt their own efforts were faltering did they invite King's SCLC to come to Chicago to forge an alliance. Chicago's black population, which in the 1950s increased by 300,000 to more than 800,000, was squeezed into an area intended for a much smaller community, blocked from expanding into white neighborhoods. While the battle in Chicago would include schools and jobs, the focus of the campaign—called the Chicago Freedom Movement—was to be discrimination in housing. "If we can break the backbone of discrimination in Chicago," said King, "we can do it in all the cities in the country." The commitment of Dr. King and the Southern Christian Leadership Conference to fight for better housing in Chicago signified more than any other development the dramatic new direction of the civil rights movement.

At a Freedom Movement rally at Soldier Field on July 10, 1966, Dr. King spoke to a crowd of 60,000 people. While he expressed his approval of the new emphasis on racial pride and a more militant activism, he warned against alienating white support. The support of middle-class whites had been essential to congressional passage of the landmark civil rights bills of 1964 and 1965 that broke the back of segregation in the South. King worried that inflammatory rhetoric and the suggestion of violence would make it much more difficult to achieve the goal of racial justice.

After the rally King led more than 5,000 marchers to city hall, where he taped the demands of the Freedom Movement to the door. In the next stage of the campaign when Freedom Movement demonstrators later marched into all-white neighborhoods to protest segregated housing, they were met by crowds of angry whites.

When King and 600 marchers, surrounded by police, entered one white neighborhood, more than 10,000 angry whites were waiting for them. SCLC's Andrew Young described the hatred he saw that day as worse than anything he had ever seen in the South. "In the South we faced mobs, but it would be a couple of hundred or even 50 or 75," he said. "The violence in the South always came from the rabble element. But these were women and children and husbands and wives coming out of their homes becoming a mob—and in some ways it was far more frightening."

The open-housing marches and the national attention they attracted resulted in negotiations between the Freedom Movement and the Chicago city government, while at the same time the city succeeded in obtaining an injunction limiting the scope of the marches. On August 26 after a 10-point settlement was reached, the Freedom Movement called a halt to further marches. The settlement committed the city to support open-housing legislation and enforce existing laws. As part of the agreement the Chicago Real Estate Board, government agencies, banks, and labor, business and religious groups pledged their support.

Some blacks thought the settlement was worthless and CORE went ahead with plans for its scheduled march to the all-white suburb of Cicero, but most blacks in the Freedom Movement were pleased, with one activist calling it "a great day."

＊　　＊　　＊

The escalation of the war in Vietnam diverted America's attention away from domestic issues like economic justice and racial equality. The issue of civil rights for black Americans, which had captured the national spotlight in the Kennedy years and the early stages of the Johnson administration, was replaced by Vietnam as the country's leading political and moral concern.

The increasingly bloody and costly war in Southeast Asia upset Dr. King and compelled him to speak out. On the same day President Johnson launched a major, sustained American air attack on North Vietnam—March 2, 1965—Dr. King called for a negotiated settlement to the conflict in a speech he gave at Howard University. In 1966 when SNCC came out against the war, King did not go along with Roy Wilkins of the NAACP, Whitney Young of the Urban League and other civil rights leaders who made a point of distancing themselves from SNCC's position.

Throughout 1965 and 1966 King included his war views in speeches and press statements, but he refrained from making a speech specifically about the war or directly criticizing the president's escalation of it. Advisers warned him not to speak out against the war for fear he might jeopardize the civil rights movement by alienating the Johnson administration. Opponents of the war were already being called communists and traitors to their country.

King worked behind the scenes to influence the SCLC position, and in April 1966 he convinced the SCLC board to take a stand against the war. That August the annual convention of the SCLC passed a resolution calling for an immediate, unilateral de-escalation of the war. Still, many of King's advisers continued to warn him against linking civil rights to the war, fearing he was letting himself get distracted from the goals of the civil rights movement.

In 1967 King took a more openly forceful stand against the war. In February he made a strong antiwar speech in Los Angeles, and on March 27 in Chicago he took part in his first antiwar march. He and the famous baby doctor, Dr. Benjamin Spock, led a march by 5,000 war protesters. He delivered a major antiwar speech at Riverside Church in New York, followed a week and a half later by a speech to more than 125,000 antiwar protesters at the Spring Mobilization march in New York City.

The *New York Times*, the *Washington Post* and other major newspapers denounced King for speaking out on foreign policy. Andrew Young said it was as if people figured it's all right for black people to be nonviolent when they're dealing with white people, but white people don't need to be nonviolent when they're dealing with brown people. He characterized the reaction of the media as a torrent of hate.

Muhammad Ali experienced the same kind of hostility when he refused to be drafted into the army. Born Cassius Marcellus Clay in Louisville, Kentucky in 1942, he had upset Sonny Liston to become the world heavyweight champion at the age of 22. The day after the fight he announced his conversion to the Muslim religion and changed his name. Later when he said, "I ain't got no quarrel with the Vietcong" and refused to be inducted into the U.S. Army for religious reasons, he was convicted and stripped of his title. In 1970, four years after the Supreme Court overturned his conviction, Ali regained his world heavyweight boxing title.

With traditional supporters dropping away, the support of the federal government waning, and more militant blacks criticizing him for not being radical enough, Dr. King continued to press for fundamental changes in American life. When Senator Robert Kennedy suggested to Marian Wright, a young lawyer, that Dr. King bring poor people to Washington to publicize the grinding poverty that afflicted the lives of millions of Americans—black and white—King liked the idea and convinced the SCLC to support it. In December 1967 he announced publicly that the SCLC planned to bring poor people of all races from different parts of the country to Washington around April 1 and have them stay in the nation's capital until America responded.

As plans for what came to be known as the Poor People's Campaign proceeded during the winter of 1968, King went to Memphis, Tennessee to speak at a rally of striking sanitation workers. In February, 1,300 of them, nearly all of them black, had gone out on strike to protest the city's sending 22 black workers home without pay because of bad weather while white workers were not sent home and got paid. The striking workers wanted the city to recognize their union. When James Lawson of the SCLC invited King to Memphis to support the strikers, King saw a chance to link the issues of economic justice and civil rights.

When King returned to Memphis on March 28 to lead a march, violence erupted along the way. Stores were damaged, 280 people were arrested, 60 people were injured and a black 16-year-old was killed by police gunfire. The FBI and some newspapers cited the eruption of violence at the march as evidence of possible violence at the Poor People's Campaign in Washington. When King left Memphis the next day and promised to return for another march, he made sure the new march would be planned and organized by the SCLC to make sure it was nonviolent.

King returned to Memphis on April 3 to confer with local leaders about the new march scheduled for April 8.

That evening at Mason Temple he gave a sermon that has come to be known as his mountain-top speech. In it Dr. King spoke about how ministers needed to be involved in social issues and how blacks should support black enterprises and institutions of good will. Then he concluded the sermon with these words:

Well, I don't know what will happen now. We've got some difficult days ahead. But it really doesn't matter with me now, because I've been to the mountaintop. And I don't mind. Like anybody, I would like to live a long life. Longevity has its place. But I'm not concerned about that now. I just want to do God's will. And He's allowed me to go up to the mountain, and I've looked over, and I've seen the promised land. I may not get there with you. But I want you to know tonight, that we as a people will get to the promised land. And I'm so happy tonight. I'm not worried about anything. I'm not fearing any man. Mine eyes have seen the glory of the coming of the Lord.

The next day—April 4, 1968—Dr. Martin Luther King, Jr. was assassinated as he stood on the balcony of the Lorraine Motel, where he and his aides were staying. Black communities across the nation exploded with grief and rage at the news of his murder. Violence erupted in 110 cities. More than 75,000 National Guardsmen were called out, and 39 people were killed.

The civil rights movement lost its soul and the nation lost a great leader. Dr. King's death and the election of Republican Richard Nixon to the presidency later in the year marked the end of one of the most important chapters in American history.

✳   ✳   ✳

After Dr. King's assassination, the civil rights movement continued to suffer the fragmentation and decline that had begun in

Soldiers directing traffic in Washington, D.C., in the aftermath of rioting that broke out after the assassination of Martin Luther King, Jr. on April 4, 1968. *(Library of Congress)*

Members of the Poor People's Campaign in Washington, D.C., walking down Connecticut Avenue on June 18, 1968. The campaign succeeded in focusing national attention on the plight of poor Americans, but soon after the tents of Resurrection City were set up on the Mall, preoccupations with the Vietnam War and presidential politics stole back the spotlight, and the "city" was razed. *(Library of Congress)*

King's last years. What once had been a mighty river during the movement's heyday of sit-ins, freedom rides, demonstrations and voter registration drives became a series of streams and brooks.

The Poor People's Campaign came to fruition four weeks after King's assassination when Ralph Abernathy, new head of the SCLC, opened the campaign by leaving Memphis for Washington with the first group of marchers. Poor people from the South, West and North moved by car, bus, foot and mule train toward the nation's capital to take up residence on the Mall near the Lincoln Memorial, where five years earlier 250,000 people had gathered to hear Dr. King. Abernathy told the marchers before they left that they must teach white America that they may be able to kill the leader but they cannot kill the dream.

In Washington, Abernathy welcomed the poor people to the makeshift tent city on the Mall called "Resurrection City," which at its peak housed 2,500 people. The poor people who converged on the nation's capital were mostly black, but they also included whites, Native Americans and Hispanics. Three weeks after Resurrection City opened the Poor People's Campaign lost one of its staunchest allies when Robert Kennedy was killed in California shortly after winning the state's June 6 presidential primary.

The campaign succeeded in making poor people visible to the rest of the country, at least for awhile, but a nation preoccupied with war and presidential politics soon lost interest. On June 24 Resurrection City was torn down and its inhabitants driven off the Mall with tear gas. Jesse Jackson, who served as the city's unofficial mayor, said that even though he felt betrayed and abandoned, he was determined to keep the struggle moving forward.

✳   ✳   ✳

After the King assassination and the Poor People's Campaign, many blacks saw the Black Panthers as a viable alternative to Dr. King's philosophy of nonviolence. "The murder of King changed the whole dynamic of the country," said Kathleen Neal Cleaver, a SNCC activist who joined the Black Panther Party. The change of mood was especially apparent in the black community, she said. "It was like, 'Well, we tried that, and that's what happened.' So even though there were many people, and many black people, who thought nonviolent change was a good thing and the best thing, nobody came out and supported it."

By late 1968 the Black Panther Party had more than 1,000 members with chapters in New York, Los Angeles and more than 20 other American cities. While Black Panther leader Huey Newton was in jail awaiting trial for the October 1967 killing of an Oakland policeman, the party organized dozens of "Free Huey" rallies and sought to link up with other groups, black and white alike.

The Panthers were not prepared for all the media attention and the police repression that suddenly thrust the party into the national spotlight, "'cause they sort of went hand in hand," said Kathleen Cleaver. "The more repression, the more media attention; the more media attention, the more repression."

The director of the FBI, J. Edgar Hoover, set out to disrupt and destroy the Black Panthers after he had already targeted SCLC,

SNCC and the Nation of Islam. On August 25, 1967, he had ordered FBI field offices to begin a new effort "to expose, disrupt, misdirect, discredit, or otherwise neutralize the activities of black nationalist, hate-type organizations and groupings, their leadership, spokesmen, membership and supporters." Originally the Black Panthers had not been on Hoover's list, but in September 1968 he declared them to be "the greatest threat" to the internal security of the country. Of the 295 counterintelligence programs the FBI directed at black groups during the 1960s, 233 targeted the Black Panthers.

In September 1968 after Huey Newton was convicted of voluntary manslaughter in the killing of the Oakland police officer and sent to prison, he advocated a number of new party programs to "serve the people," including several free health clinics and a free breakfast program for children.

In 1968 some Panther members ran for political office as candidates of the Peace and Freedom Party, a biracial party founded in California. Eldridge Cleaver, who ran for president, received almost 200,000 votes nationwide. However, infiltration by FBI informants, police repression and waning interest by the media soon led to the party's decline. The police murder of Panthers Fred Hampton and Mark Clark in Chicago in December 1969 brought the period of Black Panther notoriety to an abrupt end.

The civil rights movement was the inspiration and model for a decade of other social protest movements—the student and antiwar movements of the late 1960s, and the women's, environmental, welfare rights and prison reform movements of the 1970s. The movement's energy and the energy of the antiwar movement that followed it played a major part in the creation of the counterculture and the "greening of America" that flowed from it. In the 1970s and 1980s the civil rights movement continued to make progress alongside and in conjunction with the other social protest movements it helped create.

Not long after the 1965 Voting Rights Act blacks began translating their civil rights gains into political victories in both the North and the South. In November 1967, Cleveland became the first major city in American history to elect a black mayor when

Democrat Carl Stokes beat his white Republican opponent by 1,679 votes, winning 95 percent of the black vote and almost 20 percent of the white vote. In 1967 there were other notable gains. Richard Hatcher was elected mayor of Gary, Indiana, and Thurgood Marshall became the first black to serve on the Supreme Court.

On the weekend of March 10–12, 1972, 8,000 blacks from around the country attended the National Black Political Convention in Gary, Indiana to forge a national consensus about future directions and goals. Delegates debated and ratified a document called the National Black Political Agenda. It recommended black congressional representation in proportion to the size of the black population, community control of schools in black neighborhoods, national health insurance, a guaranteed minimum annual income, a bill of rights for prisoners and the abolition of capital punishment.

In many ways the convention marked a political coming of age for the black community as it began sensing its electoral strength at the local, state and national levels. The black congressional delegation was already beginning to flex its muscles. After the deaths of Hampton and Clark in late 1969, eight black members of Congress went to Chicago to hold a special congressional hearing on the killings.

In 1970, 12 members of what would soon be called the Black Congressional Caucus sought to present President Nixon with black grievances, but he refused to meet with them. However, after they boycotted the president's State of the Union address in January 1971, Nixon agreed to meet with them. The growth of the Black Congressional Caucus is a measure of just how much political power blacks have achieved in 20 years. Today, although financially troubled, the Black Caucus—40 strong—is a powerful voice in Washington, speaking on behalf of minorities and poor people against those who would deny them federal assistance.

Black mayors have now been elected in most of the nation's largest cities—New York, Los Angeles, Chicago, Philadelphia, Detroit, Atlanta, Newark and many others. Black voters have also played a pivotal role in the election of Democratic presidents—Jimmy Carter in 1976 and Bill Clinton in 1992. Jesse Jackson made history with two strong runs for the Democratic nomination for president in 1984 and 1988. In 1988 when he came in second, he received more votes in the primaries than the nominee Walter Mondale did in 1984.

"We've started further back than anybody else," Jackson said. "After all, the Constitution designates African descendants as three-fifths human. No immigrant group had to face that mathematical equation. . . . There was another hundred years of legal apartheid, the segregation in this country. After all of this struggle—public accommodations, equal access and protection under the law, as opposed to separate but equal—came the right to vote."

Calling the right to vote "the most fundamental shift from slaveship en route to championship," Jackson sees the great potential of this growing black political clout. "Within our lifetime this ongoing struggle will have an African-American as nominee of a major political party. Indeed, as president of the United States of America."

*   *   *

Many blacks see the gains of recent decades as fragile and in some cases illusory, affecting the lives of the black middle class much more than inner-city blacks trapped in the crime-ridden ghettos of America's big cities. Moreover, there has been a white backlash against equal opportunity programs, affirmative action and quotas designed to consolidate and promote black progress.

Racial incidents continue to plague college campuses and big cities. Two incidents in New York illustrated the pervasiveness of the problem. In 1986 whites attacked three black men who found themselves in the predominantly white Howard Beach section of Queens (one of the victims, Michael Griffith, died). Three years later 16-year-old Yusuf Hawkins was killed when he went to a white neighborhood in Brooklyn to answer a classified ad for a used car.

According to Elaine Jones, director-counsel of the NAACP, the dream rooted in the constitutional principle that all people are equal under the law has begun to dry up in recent years. She points to several pieces of evidence to back up her claim that the national engine of racial equality has stalled.

Blacks who apply for mortgages are turned down at a rate twice that of whites. One out of every nine black families earns less than $5,000 a year. In one state, Indiana, the median household

Reverend Jesse Jackson, a former aide to Martin Luther King, Jr., made two strong runs for the Democratic nomination for president, in 1984 and 1988. He has said, "Within our lifetime this ongoing struggle will have an African-American as nominee of a major political party. Indeed, as president of the United States of America." *(Library of Congress)*

income in the 1980s dropped 16 percent for blacks compared to 1 percent for whites. Newborn black infants in Tennessee are more likely to die than infants in many poor countries. During the 12 Reagan-Bush years only two of 115 judges appointed to the federal appeals court were black.

While the civil rights movement has done much to improve the life of blacks in America, there is still a long way to go before racial equality is achieved.

CHAPTER EIGHT NOTES

page 111   "I am appalled . . . Over and over . . . big cities." **Voices**, pp. 297–298.

page 112   "If we can break . . . country." James R. Ralph, Jr., **Northern Protest: Martin Luther King, Jr., Chicago, and the Civil Rights Movement**. Cambridge, MA: Harvard University Press, p. 43.

page 112   "In the South . . . frightening." **Voices**, pp. 312–313.

page 114   "I ain't . . . Vietcong." *Barry Denenberg,* **The Story of Muhammad Ali**. New York: Dell, 1990, p. 57.

pages 115–   "Well, I don't know . . . the coming of the Lord."
116   Quoted in **Bearing**, p. 621.

page 118   "The murder . . . It was like . . . supported it . . . 'cause they sort of . . . more repression." **Voices**, p. 514.

pages 118–   "to expose . . . membership and supporters." Quoted
119   in **Civil Rights**, p. 145.

page 121   "We've started . . . After all . . . to vote . . . the most fundamental shift . . . Within our lifetime . . . America." **Voices**, pp. 662–663.

CHRONOLOGY

1787   September 17. U.S. Constitution declares that, for purposes of taxation and representation, a slave counts as three-fifths of a person

1896   May 18. Supreme Court in *Plessy v. Ferguson* rules that segregation is constitutional

1909   National Association for the Advancement of Colored People (NAACP) founded

1914   Marcus Garvey founds Universal Negro Improvement Association

1939   April 9. Marian Anderson, denied permission to sing in Constitution Hall in Washington, D.C. gives outdoor concert at Lincoln Memorial on Easter Sunday

1942   Congress of Racial Equality (CORE) founded by James Farmer and others in Chicago

1947   CORE sends first Freedom Rider group to test Supreme Court ban on segregation in interstate travel

Jackie Robinson becomes first black to play major league baseball

1948   President Truman orders end of segregation in armed forces

1954   May 17. Supreme Court in *Brown v. Topeka Board of Education* rules that racial segregation in public schools is unconstitutional

1955   December 1. Arrest of Rosa Parks for refusing to give up her seat to a white man leads to Montgomery bus boycott (December 1955 to December 1956)

1957   January 10–11. Southern Christian Leadership Conference (SCLC) founded with Dr. Martin Luther King, Jr. as president

September 24. President Eisenhower orders federal troops to Little Rock, Arkansas to prevent interference with the integration of Central High School

1960 February 1. Students in Greensboro from North Carolina Agricultural and Technical College stage sit-in at Woolworth lunch counter; movement spreads to other southern cities

April 15–17. Student Nonviolent Coordinating Committee (SNCC) organized

1961 May 4. CORE launches series of Freedom Rides into the South

1962 October 1. James Meredith enters University of Mississippi under federal protection

1963 March–June. Dr. King and the SCLC wage civil rights campaign in Birmingham, Alabama

June 13. Medgar Evers assassinated in Jackson, Mississippi

August 28. More than 250,000 people participate in March on Washington

September 14. Bombing of Sixteenth Street Baptist Church in Birmingham kills four young black girls

1964 July 2. President Johnson signs Civil Rights Act

June–August. Massive voter registration drive ("Freedom Summer") launched in Mississippi

Mississippi Freedom Democratic Party organized during Freedom Summer

1965 February 21. Malcolm X assassinated in New York City

March 21–25. Dr. King leads voting rights march from Selma to Montgomery, Alabama

August 6. President Johnson signs Voting Rights Act

August 11–16. Blacks riot in Watts section of Los Angeles

1966	June. Stokely Carmichael, head of SNCC, calls for "black power"
	July–August. Dr. King takes his southern-based civil rights campaign north to Chicago
	October. Huey Newton and Bobby Seale form their own Black Panther Party in Oakland, California
1967	Dr. King speaks out more forcefully against U.S. policy in Vietnam
	June 13. Thurgood Marshall, former NAACP lawyer, nominated as first black associate justice of the U.S. Supreme Court. He is sworn in on October 2.
	November. Carl Stokes of Cleveland, Ohio and Richard Hatcher of Gary, Indiana are first blacks to be elected mayors of major American cities
1968	April 4. Dr. King is assassinated in Memphis
	May–June 24. Ralph Abernathy, King's successor as head of the SCLC, leads Poor People's March on Washington, D.C.
1972	March 10–12. National Black Political Convention held in Gary, Indiana
1977	Andrew Young, former aide of Dr. King, becomes first black to serve as U.S. ambassador to the United Nations
1984	Jesse Jackson seeks the Democratic presidential nomination
1986	January 15. Birthday of Martin Luther King, Jr. celebrated as a federal holiday for the first time
1990	November. Douglas Wilder of Virginia becomes the first black governor of any state since Reconstruction; David Dinkins becomes the first black mayor of New York City

FURTHER READING

Blumberg, Rhoda Lois. *Civil Rights: The 1960s Freedom Struggle* (rev. ed.). Boston: G.K. Hall, 1991.

Branch, Taylor. *Parting the Waters: America in the King Years, 1954–1963*. New York: Simon & Schuster, 1988.

Bullard, Sara. *Free at Last: A History of the Civil Rights Movement and Those Who Died in the Struggle*. New York: Oxford University Press, 1993.

Carmichael, Stokely, and Charles V. Hamilton. *Black Power: The Politics of Liberation in America*. New York: Random House, 1967.

Carson, Clayborne. *In Struggle: SNCC and the Black Awakening of the 1960s*. Cambridge: Harvard University Press, 1981.

Chappell, David L. *Inside Agitators: White Southerners in the Civil Rights Movement*. Baltimore: Johns Hopkins University Press, 1994.

Clark, E. Culpepper. *The Schoolhouse Door: Segregation's Last Stand at the University of Alabama*. New York: Oxford University Press, 1993.

Eagles, Charles W. *Outside Agitator: Jon Daniels and the Civil Rights Movement in Alabama*. Chapel Hill: University of North Carolina Press, 1993.

Franklin, John Hope, and Alfred A. Moss Jr. *From Slavery to Freedom: A History of African Americans* (6th ed.). New York: Knopf, 1988.

Garrow, David J. *Bearing the Cross: Martin Luther King, Jr. and the Southern Christian Leadership Conference*. New York: Vintage, 1988.

———. *Protest at Selma: Martin Luther King, Jr. and the Voting Rights Act of 1965*. New Haven: Yale University Press, 1978.

Greenberg, Jack. *Crusaders in the Courts: How a Dedicated Band of Lawyers Fought for the Civil Rights Revolution*. New York: Basic Books, 1994.

Hampton, Henry, and Steve Fayer. *Voices of Freedom: An Oral History of the Civil Rights Movement from the 1950s through the 1980s*. New York: Bantam, 1990.

Haskins, James. *The March on Washington*. New York: HarperCollins, 1993.

Holt, Len. *The Summer That Didn't End: The Story of the Mississippi Civil Rights Project of 1964*. New York: Da Capo Press, 1992.

Huckaby, Elizabeth. *Crisis at Central High: Little Rock, 1957–58*. Baton Rouge: Louisiana State University Press, 1980.

King, Martin Luther, Jr. *Stride Toward Freedom: The Montgomery Story*. New York: Harper & Row, 1958.

Levine, Ellen. *Freedom's Children: Young Civil Rights Activists Tell Their Own Stories*. New York: Putnam, 1993.

Malcolm X. *By Any Means Necessary* (2nd ed.). New York: Pathfinder, 1992.

Malcolm X, and Alex Haley. *The Autobiography of Malcolm X*. New York: Grove Press, 1965.

Meier, August, and Elliott M. Rudwick. *CORE: A Study in the Civil Rights Movement 1942–1968*. New York: Oxford University Press, 1973.

Meredith, James H. *Three Years in Mississippi*. Bloomington: Indiana University Press, 1966.

Mills, Kay. *This Little Light of Mine: The Life of Fannie Lou Hamer*. New York: Dutton, 1993.

Mills, Nicolaus. *Like a Holy Crusade: Mississippi 1964—The Turning Point of the Civil Rights Movement in America*. Chicago: Ivan R. Dee, 1992.

Murray, Paul T. *The Civil Rights Movement: References and Resources*. Boston: G.K. Hall, 1993.

Myers, Walter Dean. *Malcolm X: By Any Means Necessary*. New York: Scholastic, 1993.

Oates, Stephen B. *Let the Trumpet Sound: A Life of Martin Luther King, Jr.* New York: Harper & Row, 1982.

Patterson, Charles. *Marian Anderson*. New York: Franklin Watts, 1988.

Pfeffer, Paula F. *A. Philip Randolph: Pioneer of the Civil Rights Movement*. Baton Rouge: Louisiana State University Press, 1990.

Ralph, James R. Jr. *Northern Protest: Martin Luther King, Jr., Chicago, and the Civil Rights Movement*. Cambridge: Harvard University Press, 1993.

Robinson, Jo Ann Gibson. *The Montgomery Bus Boycott and the Women Who Started It*. Knoxville: University of Tennessee Press, 1987.

Rummel, Jack. *Malcolm X*. New York: Chelsea House, 1989.

Siegel, Beatrice. *The Year They Walked: Rosa Parks and the Montgomery Bus Boycott*. New York: Four Winds Press, 1992.

Washington, James M., ed. *A Testament of Hope: The Essential Writings and Speeches of Martin Luther King, Jr.* San Francisco: Harper & Row, 1986.

Weisbrot, Robert. *Freedom Bound: A History of America's Civil Rights Movement*. New York: Norton, 1990.

Wexler, Sanford. *The Civil Rights Movement: An Eyewitness History*. New York: Facts On File, 1993.

Whitfield, Stephen J. *A Death in the Delta: The Story of Emmett Till*. New York: Free Press, 1988.

Williams, Juan. *Eyes on the Prize: America's Civil Rights Years*. New York: Viking, 1987.

Woodward, C. Vann. *The Strange Career of Jim Crow*. New York: Oxford University Press, 1974.

I N D E X

Page numbers in *italic* indicate illustrations.

Goodman/Chaney/Schwerner found murdered by 78–79
King surveillance conducted by 51
and Poor People's Campaign violence 115
SCLC surveillance conducted by 51
Selma marchers protected by 88
Fellowship of Reconciliation (FOR) 6, 34–37
filibustering 66
firearms *see* guns
fire hoses 59
First Continental Congress 1
Florida 3
FOR *see* Fellowship of Reconciliation
Fort McClellan, Alabama 59
Fourteenth Amendment 3–4, 10, 12
Franklin, John Hope 1
"freedom now" 106
"Freedom Party" 76
freedom rides v, 6, 40–45, 47–51, 82, 117, 125
Freedom Summer 77–82, 126
Freedom Vote 76–77
"Free Huey" rallies 108, 118
free states 2
funeral homes 48

G

Gaines, Lloyd 11–12
Gandhi, Mohandas 6, 23, 35, 68
Garvey, Marcus 4, 95, 125
Gary, Indiana 120, 127
Georgia *see* Albany, Georgia; Atlanta, Georgia
Ghana 102
"global black thinking" 102
Goldwater, Barry 79
Goodman, Andrew 77–80
gradualism 9
graduate schools 12
grandfather clause 75
Gray, Fred 23
Great Society 111
Green, Ernest 30
Greensboro, North Carolina 33–34, 126
Greenwood, Mississippi 106
Gregory, Dick 69
Greyhound Bus Company 36, 42
Griffith, Michael 121
guns 107–108

H

hajj 102
Hamer, Fannie Lou 80–82, *81*
Hampton, Fred 119, 120
Harlem (New York City neighborhood) *see* New York City
Hatcher, Richard 120, 127
Hawkins, Yusuf 121
health care 110, 120
Heifetz, Jascha 5
Henry, Aaron 76
Heschel, Abraham 88
Heston, Charlton 69
Hicks, James 6
Hispanics 118
holidays 127
Holt Street Baptist Church (Montgomery, Alabama) 20

homosexuality 67
Hoover, J. Edgar 51, 118–119
Horne, Lena 69
hotels 64
House of Representatives, U.S. 2
housing vi, 39, 108, 110, 111–113
Houston, Charles 10–11, 14
Howard Beach (New York City neighborhood) *see* New York City
Howard University (Washington, D.C.) 5, 6, 10, 113
Hulett, John 105, 106
Hurok, Sol 5

I

ICC *see* Interstate Commerce Commission
Ickes, Harold 5
"I Have a Dream" (King speech) 70–72
ILGWU *see* International Ladies Garment Workers Union
incomes 65, 120, 123
Indiana 121, 123
infant death rate 123
insurance 120
integration of schools *see* schools
Interior, U.S. Department of the 5
International Ladies Garment Workers Union (ILGWU) 69
Interstate Commerce Commission (ICC) 48
Islam 95, 114 *see also* Nation of Islam

J

Jackson, Mississippi
Evers murder 126
freedom rider arrests 44
Freedom Summer preparations 77
March Against Fear 106
state fair boycott 60
Jackson, Jesse 118, 120–121, *122,* 127
Jackson, Jimmy Lee 85
Javits, Jacob 84
Jemison, T. J. 22
Jewish Theological Seminary 88
"Jim Crow" laws 2–3
jobs vi, 4, 108, 110, 112
"Jobs for Negroes" campaign 4
Johnson, Frank 86–87
Johnson, Lyndon B.
antipoverty programs 111
Civil Rights Act of 1964 78, 126
as Kennedy vice president 40, 66
Mississippi Freedom Democratic Party opposed by 79–82
presidency and civil rights vi
sees parents of missing civil rights workers 78
Vietnam War escalation 113
Voting Rights Act of 1965 85–87, 90–92, 105, 126
Jones, Elaine 121
"Journey of Reconciliation" 6
Justice Department, U.S. 42, 53, 78, 86

K

Katzenbach, Nicholas 53–54, 62, *63*

Kennedy, John F.
    Albany Movement support 50
    assassination 101
    Birmingham crisis intervention 59–60
    civil rights bill submission 63–64, 78
    freedom riders' protection from violence 42
    inaugural address 39
    March on Washington misgivings 66
    presidency and civil rights vi
    presidential campaign 38–39
    University of Alabama desegregation role
        62–64
    University of Mississippi desegregation role
        53–54
Kennedy, Robert F. 39, 42–44, 66, 114, 118
King, A. D. 57, 59
King, Coretta Scott 39, 90, 103
King, Edwin 76
King Jr., Martin Luther
    as Albany Movement supporter 49–51
    assassination 115–116
    in Atlanta sit-in 39
    Birmingham desegregation campaign
        55–60, 56, 126
    in Chicago Freedom Movement 112–113,
        127
    FBI surveillance 51
    as freedom rides supporter 43–44
    holiday for 127
    imprisonment 57–58
    Lawson meeting 35
    "Letter from a Birmingham Jail" 57–58
    Malcolm X on 103
    as March on Washington planner 65–68
    March on Washington speech ("I Have a
        Dream") 70–72
    James Meredith visited in hospital by 106
    as Montgomery bus boycott leader v, 19–25,
        20
    "Mountain-Top" speech 115–116
    as Nashville Student Movement supporter
        38
    Nobel Peace Prize to 83
    as nonviolence advocate 23, 93
    as SCLC founder 25, 125
    in Selma voting rights campaign/march
        83–90, 126
    as Vietnam War opponent 113–114, 127
    at Voting Rights Act signing (1965) 90
Koran (book) 102
Korean War 35
Ku Klux Klan 26, 59, 80, 90, 95, 104

L

labor, organized 47, 65
Lancaster, Burt 69
Lawndale, Mississippi 78
law schools 11–12
Lawson, James 34–37, 37, 115
Lee, Herbert 52
legislation, federal see Civil Rights Act of 1964;
    Civil Rights Act of 1991; Voting Rights Act of
    1965; Voting Rights Act of 1982
legislation, state 26 see also "Jim Crow" laws
"Letter from a Birmingham Jail" (Martin Luther
    King Jr.) 57–58

"Letter From a Selma Jail" (Martin Luther King
    Jr.) 84
Lewis, John 35, 41, 67, 86, 94, 105
Lewis, Rufus 19
libraries 3, 36
Lincoln, Abraham 2, 9, 66, 90
Lincoln Memorial (Washington, D.C.) 4, 5, 68,
    117, 125
liquor stores 48
Liston, Sonny 114
literacy tests 2, 75
Little, Earl 95
Little, Louise 95
Little, Malcolm see Malcolm X
Little, Reginald 98
Little, Wilfred 98
Little Rock, Arkansas see Central High School
Liuzzo, Viola 90, 104
Lomax, Louis 37
Looby, Z. Alexander 38
Lorraine Motel (Memphis, Tennessee) 116
Los Angeles, California
    black mayor elected 120
    CORE chapter set up 6
    Watts riot 107, 111, 126
Louisiana 3, 22
Lowenstein, Allard 75–76
Lowndes County, Alabama 104–107
Lowndes County Freedom Organization
    (LCFO) 105, 107
lunch counters 39, 52, 57, 59, 83, 126
lynchings 3, 7, 9, 10, 51–52, 60, 95

M

Malcolm X
    assassination 103, 126
    CORE/SNCC influenced by 104
    death threats against 101
    early life 94–97
    imprisonment 97
    Mecca pilgrimage 102
    as militant black nationalist 96, 99–101, 106,
        111
    in Nation of Islam 97–99
    Nation of Islam exit 101–102
    Selma address 102
March Against Fear 106
March on Washington for Jobs and Freedom v,
    65–72, 67, 71, 88, 94, 100, 126
Margold, Nathan 10
Marion, Alabama 85
Marshall, Burke 59
Marshall, Thurgood 11, 12, 13, 14–15, 53, 120,
    127
martial law 44
Martin Luther King Jr. Day (holiday) 127
Maryland, University of (College Park) 11
mayors 119–120, 127
McComb County, Mississippi 52, 76
Mecca (Saudi Arabia) 102
Memphis, Tennessee
    King assassination 115–116, 127
    March Against Fear 106
    segregation 7
Meredith, James 52–54, 55, 60, 80, 106, 126
Meridian, Mississippi 78